T0354661

NOVILLE Outpost *to* BASTOGNE

And other experiences with the 20th Armored Infantry Battalion, 10th Armored Division, Patton's Third Army.

BY DON ADDOR

www.trafford.com
North America & international
toll-free: 1 888 232 4444 (USA & Canada)
fax: 812 355 4082

PFC Donald J. Addor – taken on leave August 1944

"Tiger" Addor after day's training exercise, Fort Gordon, Ga.

WE GET ORDERS TO MOVE OUT

The day that it all started was, I think, either December 15th or 16th. The year was 1944. It was also the day that I received my first Christmas package from my home back in Washington, D.C. Among the Christmas cookies and cakes was a long sprig of evergreen with a bright red ribbon tied into a big bow at one end. A note was attached to explain that it was from one of the bushes in front of my home on Geranium Street in North West, D.C. The note also told me that it was cut from "above Mike's high water line." Mike was a big Irish setter that belonged to the neighbors across the street, but spent much of his time at our house and over the years this big reddish dog had become a good friend.

I hung the greenery on the front of the half-track and it looked nice hanging there. It was the only touch of Christmas anywhere around. When one is in combat one doesn't have time to think about what day it is to say nothing about holidays yet to come. However, word from home had made me realize that Christmas was not far off. I made my way over to Battalion Headquarters to see what I was going to be doing on the wet, soggy day. It had been raining almost every day since we had landed in France and I was wondering if the sun was ever going to come out. At Headquarters I passed out the cookies and cake and checked out the rest of my package. In the bottom was a pair of long wool socks in a fancy plaid pattern. I had asked for some warm socks in my last letter and here they were. They reminded me of the socks Dad had worn with his golfing knickers back in the Thirties. Not very GI, but they were warm and for once my feet were warm.

I was tucking my pants into my newly issued combat boots, when the sergeant told me to get over and relieve the guy on the telephone switchboard. This was an old battered olive drab box sitting on a stand over in the corner of the room. The wooden box had a mess of wires coming into its back and round black tubes with brass plugs on the end coming out of the front. These were in rows over a similar row of holes. I had seen bigger versions of switchboards in movies, but this looked like something left over from World War I. Maybe it was. Some of our machine guns had 1918 and '19 dates on them.

However, the important thing was that it worked. We used telephone instead of radio because they were a lot harder for the enemy to listen in on. The radios had crystals that were changed every day to vary frequencies, but the Germans usually knew what these secret wavelengths were before we did. To listen in on a telephone conversation they had to crawl through our lines and splice into the wiring. Not only was it dangerous to do, but also one could usually tell by the change of tone if a tap had been made. Laying all of that wire out every place we went, even on patrols behind the lines, was a Hell of a job, but worth it.

I was sitting there enjoying how warm and comfortable my feet felt in my Christmas socks when one of the "holes" buzzed me. I answered. It was for the Major so I made the right connections and this is about how the conversation went. (It was standard procedure for the operator to listen in unless he was ordered off. This was kind of a safety check to make sure everything was OK.) The calling voice with a strong note of authority said, "Major, how soon can you be ready to move out?" The Major said, "In an hour or two." The voice said, "Make that 45 minutes!" The Major's answer was "Yes, Sir!" and the entire 20th Armored Infantry Battalion began to haul ass in double time. It was a mad house of roaring tanks, half-tracks and trucks, a lot of cussing and bitching, but we were ready to roll right on time.

This was how 20th AIB of the 10th Armored Division ended their brief rest period in Battalion reserve. We had only started to get the supplies and replacements needed from our drive down the Moselle-Saar Valley that had ended in the capture of the ancient city Metz. It was said that this was the first time in 500 years that heavily fortified town had been taken. We had also been the first of Patton's Third Army to enter Germany. We had needed that "rest" to get back up to fighting strength, but we would have to made do with what we had once again. No one had told us why or where we were going, just to get going, but we knew we were heading north.

We knew nothing of Bastogne or about the German "break through." Nor did we have any idea that we were heading into the biggest land battle ever fought. In fact when we saw that the road signs were indicating that we were heading to the rear through towns that we had fought from the enemy not too long ago, we actually thought just maybe we were heading for that dream break, R & R in Paris, that wonderful city full of booze and women. However, this dream didn't last very long for we soon began to get hints that we were heading farther north to stop some kind of counter attack.

During each break on our "march" we hear and increasing amount of talk from civilians who had come out into the rain to stand at the edge of the road in each village about a big attack by the Germans. They asked us what we knew about Nazi paratroopers dropping behind the line and about Tiger tanks and new weapons overrunning our lines. Nobody had told us about any big attack so we just considered it a part of a German propaganda broadcast. Axis Sally had often broadcast such bull. However, the more we traveled along this muddy road the more the natives asked these questions and the more worried their voices sounded and the more anxious their faces looked.

Anyhow we were used to counter attacks. They are a part of the tactics of war. Our armored infantry units had a Hell of a lot more firepower than the regular infantry and we had often been shifted to another spot in the front where our armor was needed to throw back the enemy. However, along toward evening, even though the signs still indicated that we were heading away from the front, we began to get the feeling that something was amiss and Paris was not our destination. We drove on into the night and finally stopped in a fairly large town, at least it was larger than the ones we had passed through so far.

Our half-track, part of Battalion Headquarters, was directed to pull in to the rear of a very large walled estate. It was some kind of place, like a mansion out of a Hollywood movie. There was a huge ornate house and acres of garden all trimmed and proper. The officers got to stay in the regular part of the house, while we the enlisted went three stories up the back stairs to the attic for our billet. This was not a bad deal for although it was far from being grand like the floors below us, it was warm and dry. In fact it seemed like Heaven after all of the wet, muddy places we had slept in since we had landed in France back in September. We were told that the place belonged to the richest man in Luxembourg. This was easy to believe.

A guard was set up to patrol around the house, and I was part of this first detail. The area around the house was a beautiful formal garden, a beautiful sight to see even at night and in the winter. My area to patrol was the rose garden. As I walked between the many rose beds contemplating what a wonderful sight and smell it would be on a warm summer day, I heard the drone of airplanes high up in the sky. I looked up, but could see nothing but the dark rainy black sky. From the sound I couldn't tell how many planes were up there. I thought, "There go some more of our bombers to blast Berlin" I wondered if there would be anything left of the city when we got there.

Then suddenly the screaming of bombs heading earthward shattered the silence of the night. As I hit the ground between the rows of roses I knew those guys up there were not on our side. I heard the bombs hit about a quarter of a mile away in the city. Almost instantly the sky was cut into patterns by tracers from our 50 caliber machineguns and dotted with exploding anti-aircraft shells. It was all over in a couple of minutes. Almost as quickly as it started all was quiet and I resumed my patrolling again, with my ears straining for a possible return of the bombers, but they never came back. The quiet was interrupted occasionally through the night by the sound of the motor of a light plane circling above in the dark sky. It was only a recon plane like the one that used to cruise over us around sunset; the one we had nicknamed "Bed Check Charlie." It bothered us a bit, but not enough to keep us from getting a good, but short night's sleep.

We were back on the road before dawn so we didn't even get a good look at our wonderful quarters. Our armored column was still traveling in the same direction and the weather was the same, wet and lousy. Mud was everywhere. It had fallen off the tires and tracks of the vehicles in front of us so that there was at least a foot of it on top of the road's hard surface. All of these vehicles plowing through this mud sent up a fine spray until every part of us was covered with mud. It seemed like mud as well as blood was all a part of war. The rain turned into a drizzle and it started to get foggy. There was a lot more talk from the side of the road about a great big German attack, but we still did not associate it with our move. However, the bombing the night before should have tipped us off, as the Germans had not made air attacks for quite sometime.

That night we crossed into Belgium and entered a large town. The talk of the civilians along our way began to hit home for we could hear the rumble of combat in the distance. From what I could see of the town in the dark it reminded me of the warehouse area down by the docks in Baltimore, Md. The order to dismount was given and I climbed out of the half-track with my bedroll in tow. We were directed into a nearby low building. It was good to get into a dry place. The inside of the building was full of large tanks or vats. I put my bedroll down with the other guys in one of the aisles. I had just stretched out and was getting ready for a good snooze, two nights in a row in a dry place; I was getting spoiled, when an officer rushed in and shouted, "Everybody back up. Outside and mount up on the double!"

Out we went on the double. I tossed my bedroll into the half-track and was told to take my place by the driver and to help him keep on the road. I was picked for this job because I have very good night vision. Some of the guys even claimed I could see in the dark. The driver fire the engine and a group of us headed out of town on a not too wide country road. Not only was it very dark, it had also gotten very foggy. I was standing up on the front seat and through the ring mount of our 50-caliber machinegun. Even leaning out as far as my body would go I could only see a few feet in from of us. Luckily we weren't the first vehicle. I couldn't see the one ahead of us, but its sound helped guide us.

Our detachment of men and vehicles had to creep through the night. The damn fog was so thick we couldn't go but a few miles per hour and ran off the road couple of times. All of a sudden we stopped. A voice from up ahead declared we were here. I looked around and wondered where here was. As I got more used to the fog I could see stone buildings along each side of the road. It was a small crossroad town. The word was that we were to hold this town and intersection at any or all costs.

THE BATTLE AT NOVILLE BEGINS

As Company B was deploying to set up defenses at the edge of town, Sarge disappeared into the building that was being set up as our Task Force headquarters. The men and tanks moving out to set up road blocks at the edge of town soon disappeared into the fog. Ready to face whatever was out there come dawn. Due to the heavy fog and the darkness of night I could not tell how big this village was, but it was definitely just a small crossroad settlement of old stone houses and barns. Sarge came back and said we were to unload into the house on the other corner from the Headquarters building. I asked him what we were supposed to do. He said just stand by over there in case the Major needed his half-track or us.

While the driver was restarting the half-track I walked over to the front of the house, at least what faced on this main road. There I found a big wide door and when I opened it there was no house, just an ancient barn. The iron rings in the wall where cattle or horses were tied were empty and the animals were long gone. Not a fresh pile of dung any place on the straw laden floor. I shut the door and walked to the corner of the building and found that it had been built on a forward side of a hill that sloped into a town. Thus the living quarters at the front were one story up while at the rear they were at ground level. The driver backed the track against the side wall about half way up the hill and we entered through a tall window.

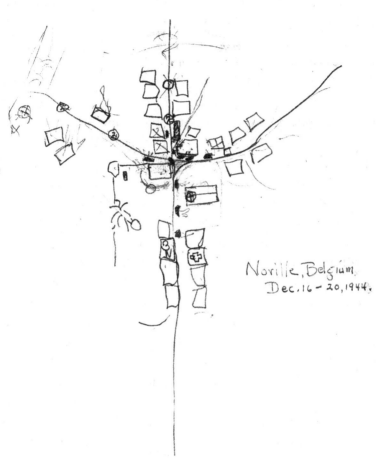

Noville, Belgium.
Dec. 16 - 20, 1944.

A map of Noville as I saw and/or remembered it. Drawn after arrival home in spring of 1945 to explain to my parents what went on.

I was handing stuff we might need through the window when a squad from B Company passed by. The leader said hi, and made some remarks about the damn fog. Before I could answer they had disappeared into the white blanket. I agreed. It sure was foggy. It was the worst damn fog I had ever seen. Couldn't see but a few feet in any direction. It must have been this bad when who ever it was described it as being as thick as pea soup. Well at least it wasn't green and maybe it would burn off when the sun came up. I checked the half-track and went in through the window.

I looked around. It was a nice home with nice furnishings. It was kind of surprising as the outside of the house was old, rough stone and was built several hundred years ago. However, the biggest surprise was to see that the dinning room table was set for dinner complete with food that appeared to be only half eaten. It was still fresh and very tempting. I had not seen such a layout since I had been home on leave. That seemed like years ago, but in reality it had only been five months ago. One thing for sure was that who ever had lived here they sure did leave in a hurry. As I said, it sure looked good, but we knew better than to eat or drink anything not Army issued.

While I was wondering where these people had gone, Sarge told someone to check out the upstairs to make sure no one was hiding up there, friend or foe. This was routine procedure. Occasionally we found some one holed up in a cellar, but usually the whole town was empty. I always wondered where and how they went. We seldom saw any of them on the roads and when we went back a few days later the residents were everywhere moving back in and already starting to repair damage. I went to the rear of the house and opened a small door. There, a few steps down, was some kind of a storage cellar. It wasn't a very big place, but it sure looked safe. Not only did it

NOVILLE OUTPOST TO BASTOGNE

have the thick stone walls of the house, but it was underground too.

I went back to the front of the house and told Sarge about it. He said, good, we'll use it for sleeping quarters. Some one had already knocked out all the glass from the large front window. This was always done to keep us from getting hit and cut by flying glass if and when shells hit outside. The first time I had to smash a perfectly good window it had seemed like useless destruction. However, it didn't take long for me to realize how dangerous these windows were. A shell had landed outside in the street just as I was entering a room and I was lucky not to have been cut as jagged pieces of glass flew about the room. Someone had also pointed out that there would be no glass left in any windows in the whole town after the battle. He was right. The fact that these windows were still intact was evidence that no one had shelled the town yet.

The machinegun from our half-track had been set up in the front window. Since we were one story up overlooking the street we would have a good field of fire. However it was too dark and foggy to tell what was out there. The guy came back down from checking the upstairs. He reported that all was clear and added that we should see the "beautiful" beds. We all had thoughts of getting a good sleep in a real bed, on a real mattress, but opted for the safety of the storage cellar. It was a natural bomb shelter.

Along one side of the cellar was a large bin of turnips. They were the very large ones, at least the size of a softball. Down where we had come from the farmers put them through a large shredder and fed them to their cattle. They also made big round loaves of bread out of the turnips. It took almost a week of aging before the bread could be eaten. Well now these turnips in their bin were going to be our bed. I spread my homemade sleeping bag over them and climbed into the bin and stretched out. Man, was it lumpy and hard. I looked around to see if there was a better spot. On the other side of this narrow room was a long row of shelves that held an assortment of jars and cans. One guy was already sleeping on the floor of the walkway, so this was it. Actually I was so tired that the lumps didn't keep me from going to sleep. I hadn't been asleep long before the pounding of exploding artillery shells woke me.

The battle had started. The enemy knew we were here and wanted us out. I tried to get back to sleep, but it was no use. It was safe here, but I could still hear the muffled sounds of the incoming artillery and feel the vibration of their blast. I rolled out of the turnip bin and ran up the short flight of wooden steps and into the living room at the front of the house. As I entered, I was hit in the face with a terrible smell. Boy! What a stink! The slight breeze that was blowing had shifted and was coming from the valley. I knew the smell. I had smelled it before. It came from the burning horses and cows trapped in their flaming barns. They were dead now, but the smell lingered on. When we could get to the barns in time we would free the animals and let them run wild. Shellfire would kill a few, but a least they had some chance of survival.

Another group of 88's slammed into town. These were close by, hitting the house next door and shaking the Hell out of the one we were in. These came from German tanks not too far away, but hidden by the heavy fog. As the shells struck, a machinegun or burp gun fired down the center of the street narrowly missing several men coming out of Battalion Headquarters. Sarge said to me, "See that! There's a sniper down there some place and no one has been able to find him. We've searched everywhere. Can't figure where the Hell he's at!" It was true B Company had sent out details that had searched every house in town and had found no one. Yet every time there was a shelling to distract us he would fire down the street again. If he had been using tracer bullets spotting would have been easy, but he was too smart for that.

The word was passed that there was a sniper in the town and care was to be taken in the area around HQ. Everyone crossed the intersection in quick dashes. He fired a lot, but as far as I know he never hit anyone. No harm was done, but it was a form of harassment and there was always the chance he might get lucky and hit someone. I had figured that the sniper fire had to be coming from a house very near us. It was one that kind of stuck out into the street a bit and would be a logical choice because it gave full field of fire down the main street. However, that house had been searched several times immediately after his firing had stopped and still no one could be found.

The assault on the town had begun in earnest so there was no time to worry about just one guy firing at us. Out on the edge of town I could hear the roar of cannon fire as our tanks fought it out with their German counterparts. This was no even battle as the German armor was far superior. Their tanks were armed with 88-millimeter guns and our Sherman's only had 75-millimeter guns and our tank destroyers only 76's. The German tanks although bigger and heavier with thick armor plate could still move faster and with wider tracks could run across wet grass lands where our tanks would sink like a rock in water. It was the skill of our tanker and their teamwork that won the battles.

I went out the window to the half-track. It was as foggy as ever, but not as dark. Dawn was breaking and I hoped that when the sun got up that it would burn away this fog. I could hardly see across the street to Battalion Headquarters so how the Hell could we see the damn Germans. After looking all around to get a better idea of what kind of town we were defending, I went back looking for some rations for breakfast. I was hoping we had some "C" rations stowed away some place, but it looked like I was going to have to make do with the "K" rations we already had in the house. Anyhow I was getting tired of the "Meat and Beans." It really wasn't that bad, but when you had it for breakfast, lunch and dinner for a month it somehow loses its appeal. There were plenty of other good kinds of this ration, but by the time they got to us at the front only the "Meat and Beans" were left.

I was about to go back through the window when I heard a commotion in the fog up the road leading out of town. I heard voices hollering in both German and English. Then the sound of boots running toward me and soon appearing out of the fog was the detail that had gone out in the dark of night to dig in at the town's edge. They stopped next to the half-track to regroup. I asked the leader what the Hell was happening and he told me this. They had dug their foxholes in a line at the top of the hill just beyond the house that I was in and waited. After some time had passed they heard some troops digging in near them, but it was too foggy to see anything. I just assumed that it was the reinforcements or replacements we had been told we were getting so I didn't bother to check. Besides, you can hear a whisper a mile away in this fog.

Well when it got lighter just a while ago I decided to see whom our friends were who had dug in with us. I stood up and looked out of my hole and was staring a damn Kraut right in the face. Well we were both so surprised that we both did what came naturally, beat it the Hell out of there. They ran back their way and we ran here! I guess they thought they were joining with some of their guys. He added we're going back now and if we see them again we'll get 'em. I could hear him cussing himself for not shooting them then and there. Strange things happen sometimes and this fog was giving us all the creeps. That small group of guys went right back up there and for two whole days held off assault after assault of von Rundstedt's best panzers. Later that day a similar thing happened to me. I was walking down the main road in the town through the thick fog and I heard someone approaching from my rear. When he got along side of me I looked over and it was a German rifle-man. He ran one way and I ran the other. It was the sudden shock of seeing the enemy right there beside me.

The Sniper Makes a Mistake

That sniper was there all day long. Every time artillery or mortar shells came screaming in to keep us pinned down, he would spray the area with several bursts from his burp gun. We had gotten much too busy throwing back attacks from the German tanks and infantry to spend any time to try and locate the lone gunman. We knew his area of fire and times he was likely to fire so we crossed that intersection with great speed. He was a pain in the ass, but I never heard that he hit anybody.

Later that night the German attacks had slacked off. I pulled a large overstuffed chair up close to the front window so I could keep my watch in comfort. We were still standing by with the Major's half-track and hadn't heard a word from over there all day. The machinegun was in the window ready to use if one of the attacks should push up the street, but right now things had quieted down with only the occasional barrage hitting here and there in the town. None too close to our post to worry much about. It sure felt good to sit down in this comfortable chair. I had a good view out of this second floor window. I could see both ways up and down the street and of course I could see the house directly across from me. The view would be a lot better if this fog would go away.

Artillery fire had struck the house across the street several times and the old stone house was burning. Although the outside of the house was made of large stones the insides of it created quite a fire. The flames reflected in the fog and gave it an orange glow. This with the flames reflecting on the wet cobblestones gave the whole area a spooky and unreal appearance. Staring into the fire over there had me mesmerized until a blast of machinegun fire yanked me back to reality. It was the sniper firing again. He was firing at some shadowy figures crossing the street down by the Headquarters building. This time we was using tracers...

What the main street of Noville looked like after the battle. It also shows why I remembered it as "No Ville" left.

He fired again and his bullets cut a burning path right in front of the window, so close it seemed that I could reach out and grab them. A few minutes passed and he fired again. This time I noticed something about the burning path of those bullets. Their trail was almost white. I asked Sarge if he noticed anything about them. He answered, "Yeah. They were right in front of the window, damn close!" I said, "I meant the color. They were almost white." He replied, "Dammed if they weren't." This meant he was very close, like only next-door. When tracer bullets leave the gun barrel they are glowing white with a slight tint of yellow. As they travel their color changes from yellow to orange and finally, just before they burn out they are red.

With him being that close I wondered why no one had been able to find him. I got up and went over by the window standing just to one side. I thought about the son-of-a-bitch and thought about him again. Finally, I said to Sarge, "The next time he fires I'm going to stick my head out to see where he is firing from." Sarge did not think this was such a good idea as I might just get my head blown away. But I figured a quick peak wouldn't be too dangerous so I readied myself for his next firing. I waited and waited and finally he fired down the street again. As the first rounds sailed by I stuck my head out and took a look at his next burst. He was firing out of the top of the peak of the roof of the next house. Any higher up and he would have been on the outside of the roof.

In the morning I reported what I had discovered. A detachment was sent over to the house and found him in a small crawl space above the ceiling in the attic. It was just enough room for a body to slide along to the side of the house where there was a small opening for ventilation. This is how one of the details described it to me later that day. He added that there was no regular door or opening, but a ceiling panel could be moved aside to get up there. I asked how they got him down and he said they didn't. They just fired through the ceiling where they thought he was. They riddled the whole length of the ceiling until blood started dripping through the bullet holes and they left his body up there. That was the end of that annoyance for good.

We might never of found him if he had not used tracer bullets. They help you sight in on a target and are fun to watch. However, it is very easy to follow those streaking bullets right back to the gun muzzle and gunner. Our machinegun ammo belts game with three different types of rounds one after the other. They were: an antipersonnel round with copper jacket and lead core; armor piercing with copper jacket and steel core; and the tracer bullet with the burning tail end. When ever there was time our gunners pulled the tracers and put in one of the other types of bullets. This way they did not give away their position, at least not as quickly. This helped, as a machine gunner was always a prime target.

Later that night after a short sleep, I was back on watch sitting in the easy chair. The shelling had been particularly bad so everyone else was down below in the storage cellar trying to get some sleep. Looking out the window at the town below everything seemed unreal. Many more houses were now burning, giving the whole town a Hellish red glow through the fog. The glow was increased by all of our trucks, half-tracks and tanks that had been hit earlier and were still burning. The artillery shells were coming in at regular intervals. Far off I could hear the pitiful sounding cries of cattle and horses trapped in a burning building somewhere out there in the thick fog.

The house across the street was still burning. There was not much left of it but a stone shell. The inner floors had collapsed and fallen in to a big pile of rubble on the first floor that was burning brightly. It looked a bit like a giant jack-o-lantern, but without a grinning mouth. Through the front door at the side of the house one of our patrol took a shortcut through the burning building. The fire gave them long dancing shadows that crossed the street in front of them. Then they disappeared into the fog. I felt like I was sitting in the balcony watching a movie on a super large screen. It seemed unreal. However, that feeling was short lived. Another round hit the house directly across the street. It hit the stone peak of the burned out building showering stone down on to the street. I said to myself, "Wow, if that peak had not been there that shell would have landed right in my lap." At the same time I realized that usually the Germans fired three shells in a sequence. I could hear the next shell coming as I bolted out of the chair and ran toward the safety of the little cellar. I was almost there when I heard the shell tear through the stone wall upstairs. I took a belly flop and nose-dived right down those steps ending up on top of someone. We heard it rip across the floor and crash into another wall.

We all hunkered down and waited for the explosion. None came. We waited about a half an hour in case the shell had a time delay fuse, but it never went off. Sarge figured all was safe so the watch upstairs resumed with caution. When daylight had gotten bright enough so we could see our way up the stairs to the second floor living quarters, Sarge and I went up to see what had happened. There was a hole in the outside wall of the front bedroom where the shell had penetrated the stone. The shell had entered just a few inches above the floor and had traveled across the room cutting the big double bed in half. It had come to rest imbedded in the room's inner wall with about six inches of ugly shell sticking out. We had been lucky! It was a dud for its blast in that position could have brought the whole house down on us.

A Lucky Captain, A Lucky Pig

Later in the day I was out in the half-track to look for some more food. It had to be K Rations as the C were long gone. So far the only thing I had found was a large carton of rubbers, condoms, prophylactics, whatever you want to call them. They sure weren't any use to us here up on the front. It had been at least a month since I'd seen anyone that even resembled a gal. Still when I went back for supplies I'd ask for hand grenades and if they were out they would give me a box of rubbers. What a waste. The only use we had found for them was to put them over our rifle or machinegun barrels to keep the rain out while the guns were not in use. I guess these had been saved just in case we got that leave in Paris.

I heard a voice hail me and ask how things were going. It was Captain Geiger walking my way from Headquarters. He was about in the center of the intersection when we heard a tank coming into town. We both stared into the fog until it emerged from the white stuff and we saw that it was one of our Sherman tanks. It pulled up beside the old burned out house and stopped. The Captain continued his walk in my direction and I was waiting to see what he wanted. Suddenly there was a loud explosion and a ball of fire passed over Geiger's head. It missed him by an inch or two at the most. It was the Sherman! It fired again and the Captain ducked. The shell passed over him and he stood up and pointed at the tank and at the same time hollering, "Get that son of a bitch! I don't' care who he is." With that he jumped over the stone wall of the churchyard.

Those shells that had just barely missed Captain Geiger plowed into a truck, half-track and some other vehicles parked across from me. They exploded and immediately burst into flames. Pieces of burning debris were falling all around me and kept me busy beating out the small fires they started. One of our tank destroyers answered the Captain's cry and let fly a round at the Sherman before it had come to a full stop. They made a direct hit but two of those in the tank tried to escape through the turret hatch. They were Germans dressed in Nazi uniforms. They didn't get very far; rifle and machinegun fire killed them before they hit the street. That was a close one. The tank was about 40 feet away and its fire had singed the grill on my half-track.

I got all the little fires in the track extinguished and headed back into the house through the window. Those other vehicles that had been hit burned the rest of the day and into the night. Captain Geiger hopped back over the wall and went on up the street like nothing had happened. He was one cool officer. This was how we learned that the Germans had captured our supply dumps and were using our weapons. We had lost three or four vehicles but no one had been killed or hurt. Word was passed to check all vehicles, even ours, to make sure they were still ours. Some Germans were even dressed in our uniforms. The fog had been bad enough, now this.

During one of the assaults that came a little later a strange thing happened. There was heavy small arms fire up and down the street as the enemy tried to push their way into town. A few doors up it was too foggy to see what was happening. I thought I heard voices calling, "Here piggy, here piggy!" I said to myself, "It must be all of this damn noise. Now I am hearing things." Then out of the fog came a little pig. It was scared to Hell and running just as fast as it could go. Its little legs kept it just under the stream of bullets being fired up and down the street. What I had heard was our guys trying to call the little fellow into safety.

The guys were firing and waving as they called, but the pig just kept on running down the center of the street. I even heard a few giving the country call of, "Souee piggy!" However, this Belgium pig would have only understood French so it did not pay much attention to the American pig call. Then suddenly it got the idea and darted into a door near me where it was grabbed and taken back into the house to safety. A big cheer went up and the men of Company B and the 101st Paratroopers rallied and drove the Germans back out of town. Most of the time a little porker like that would have wound up being served by the Company Mess. However, everyone agreed that the little fellow had been through enough so he became sort of a pet for the next couple of days. When we pulled out of Noville he was let go in the woods where he would have a chance of surviving.

Saving this little critter gave our morale a big boost. It was a lucky pig. One of the nasty sights of war was the sight of dead animals lying along the road or out in the fields. I know I will carry the vision of bloated horses and cows scattered here and there with me for a long time. We had been lucky, as our combat had started in the fall when the weather was cool. On a couple of days when it had warmed up the stink had been sickening. Whenever we were able, we opened the barns and let the cattle and horses out. Most of them were chained to rings in the barn's ancient stone walls, but occasionally the animals were in stalls. When we turned them loose they ran off and formed small herds that roamed the countryside until their owners returned and rounded them up. They weren't free from danger in the battle zone, but had a heck of a better chance of survival than when they were confined in a building.

I Bag Me a Tiger

Sarge was looking out of the front window and over toward the Headquarters building. Suddenly he shouted, "Hey, look at that. There's a mess of 101st Paratroopers over there at Headquarters!" I rushed to the window with the rest of the guys to have a look and sure enough there were a sizeable number of Troopers milling around the Headquarters building, both inside and out. They were talking to members of our Company B as they moved into the building. The same thought struck all at the same time. Oh boy, this must be our relief, our replacement that they said would be coming. Now we could leave this damn place and get back to our R and R. We had been told to hold until relieved and here they were!

Sarge asked for some one to go over and see what was happening. I volunteered and went out the window and across the street. The area was crowded with paratroopers and our guys. I sure hoped this was our relief. It sure looked like it. I squeezed through the door and found myself inside. I looked around for someone I knew, but it was so crowded and dusty I couldn't see much of anything. The clouds of dust were coming off the floor where mud had dropped and dried out. The many combat boots trampling over it now caused the choking dust. I was trying to push my way back to the Lieutenant's office when a soldier from Company B came rushing in from the back of the building shouting, "Tiger, Tiger. There's a Tiger tank rolling into town blowing up everything!"

Everybody headed for the basement door for the protection of the cellar below. I headed in that direction, but I was stopped by the many trying to get through that small door all at once. I thought, "Do I really want to be down there?" That was a good place to get buried alive and a Tiger tank had the firepower to bring this building down. I'm no hero type, but I'm also not of the mind to stick my head in the sand and wait for my ass to be blown away. I'd rather go down making some kind of resistance even if it was just throwing rocks. With this in mind I turned around and headed for the back door to take a look at the Tiger. I looked out the door and down the narrow blacktop road, but all I could see was the white blanket of fog that still covered the town and countryside. I shrugged my shoulders and wondered what had gotten into that GI. I turned around and there he was. I pointed down the road and said there's not a damn thing down there but fog.

He said, "Not there." Where I had pointed. "There!" And he pointed along the side of the building. There it was not 25 feet away. The biggest, meanest looking son-of-a-bitch I had ever seen. I could have spit on it if my mouth had not gone dry all of a sudden. I went back into the room looking for something to throw at it. I saw a bazooka leaning against the wall and went for it. Now the only experience I had ever had with a bazooka was way back in basic training and that was just a couple of shots for familiarization. I knew how it worked with two people, but that was all. Not only that, but this was a newer model that folded in half for easier carrying. The one I had fired was just one long pipe. I grabbed it and was trying to figure out how to get it into firing condition when a voice started giving me instructions. I looked up and it was a soldier from Company B. I asked him if it was his weapon and he answered yes. I tossed it to him and picked up a bag of rocket shells telling him to follow me.

He came. This was good as normally it takes two persons to fire a bazooka, a gunner and a loader. I remembered how to load and he knew how to gun. Just outside the door we dropped to the ground close up to the stone wall that ran from the building down along the side of the road and into the fog. We looked over the wall and there it was bigger than life. I could have thrown the bazooka shells and hit it with ease. That wouldn't have been very effective. Actually a bazooka was not very effective against a Tiger tank. Their armor was too thick, but we were up close, very close, so maybe we had a chance to at least stop its forward progress.

On the other side of the wall right in front of us was a burning half-track. The flames from it shot up in front of us giving us good concealment. Also the road on the other side of the wall was a good bit lower than our side, so we had a clear field of fire over the half-track and through the flames. I pulled a shell out of the bandoleer while (I never knew his name so I'll just call him Joe.) Joe aimed the bazooka over the wall at the tank. I pulled the pin, shoved it to the rear end of the barrel and wrapped the little wire around the contact spring. This done, I said a short prayer and signaled Joe with a pat on his back that everything was ready. He fired. What I had done must have been OK as the shell streaked out and hit the side of the Tiger. It exploded but no damage was done.

The armor plating was too thick where it hit. It did get the attention of those inside of the Tiger and it stopped. As I loaded another round the turret started to swing back and forth as they looked for what had caused the noise. This time Joe's shot hit in a different place, but the shell bounced off with out exploding and rolled into the street. The Germans inside that tank now knew someone on their right and up close was firing at them. The Tiger tank began to back slowly out of town foot by foot as they looked for us. I loaded a third round and Joe fired. This one also bounced off the tank without exploding. Joe looked around at me. I shook my head and showed him the safety pin in my hand. I was out of shells. They come in a three pack, or at least these did. I told Joe to stay put I was going for more ammo. I crawled to the door just a few feet away.

The sun shines through the roof of the church in Noville. Not much left, but the cross still hangs over the altar.

When I got there I met a couple of guys from Company B who were in the doorway watching Joe and me and that big old ugly Tiger tank. I told them to get the bazooka ammo back in the room and to take it out of its "wrapping" and hand it out the door to me. I also told them to pull the contact wire out loose so all I had to do was pull the pin, shove it in the bazooka and wrap the wire. I was back at my loader position and shoved another shell in. Joe fired. This time it exploded, but hit the heavy sloping armor on the front of the tank. It didn't phase the tank at all. The guys passed me the shells. I loaded and Joe fired. We fired eleven shells at that big monster as it slowly moved backward with that big "88" gun swinging back and forth looking for a target. That was us. I guess you could say we had the closest thing one could get to an automatic bazooka.

It didn't seem to matter if the shells just bounced off without going off or if they exploded. It didn't phase that big hunk of steel at all. I might just as well have been throwing rocks at it. They had backed down the road far enough that the flames from the burning half-track no longer hid us. In addition, a sniper from across the intersection was firing at us with tracers. He could not hit us because of the corner of the building that stuck out into his field of fire. His bullets chiseled away at the stonework sending showers of dust and chips in front of us. Actually he was not trying to hit us as much as he was trying to point us out to his comrades in the tank. The tank commander must have seen where those tracers were pointing as the big tank's tracks ground through the road, as it swung around to face us. All this time I had been loading and Joe had been firing. We must have fired at least fourteen rounds with no results. Now that big gun was pointing right at us. The tank fired but the gunner had his elevation too high and he blew away a big section of the building's roof up above our heads. As we were being showered with debris I shoved a shell into the bazooka and told Joe to fire and get the Hell out of here.

He fired and the shell exploded under that "88's" barrel, that small slit where the gun entered the turret. The gunner had been lowering his elevation and the barrel stopped its downward movement with a sudden jerk! I said, "Hey Joe, I think we got the bastard. Fire one more in the same place." I had activated the rocket and was about to run it home when there was a loud blast above my head and the concussion flattened me out on the hard ground. I was out for a couple of minutes and when I came to I was still holding the bazooka shell in my fist. The business end of it was bent over for it had hit the wall when I was thrown down. Both Joe and I thanked God that it was a dud. I looked up and was staring at the muzzle of one of the long guns of our TDs.

It had fired right over our heads and made sure that the tank was out of commission. Then I noticed there was a lieutenant standing by looking down at me. His mouth and lips were moving, but I could not hear what he was saying. In fact I could not hear anything at all but a tremendous ringing and roaring in my ears from that muzzle blast. Someone gave me a hand and helped me to my feet and into the building just as another one of our Tank Destroyers rolled into the backyard and stopped next to the one already there. Both started firing into the fog and knocked out another Tiger tank that had been just a short distance behind the first. These two tanks that had now started to burn were knocked out right in the center of the narrow road where they made an excellent road block. No other tanks could sneak into town by this road.

When the Lieutenant and I got into the building he shook my hand an helped me dust the dirt and debris off my uniform. He was still talking. Finally enough of my hearing came back so I could make out what he was saying. First he apologized for firing over our heads. He said at the time he could not tell if the tank was knocked out or not. He added that the "88" was quickly getting him and us in its sights, so he fired. He took out a small notebook and wrote down my name and outfit. He also got information about what had happened from Joe, me, and some of the GIs who had been watching. He came back and told me he was going to write Joe and me up for the Silver Star.

I hadn't gone out there looking for any medals. I had done it more or less to save my ass, but a Silver Star did sound nice. Mom and Dad would be very proud. I suddenly remembered what I had come over for. I found the Lieutenant who worked in Major Desobry's office and asked him if the 101st Paratroopers were relieving us. He said Hell no, or something like that. They were just here to reinforce us. We were to hold this road junction and town as long as we could, at any cost. They will let us know if and when we could pull back to Bastogne. Our job was to keep holding the Germans back until they could complete the defenses around Bastogne. That was the first time I had heard of that town's name. I'd seen it on road signs, but that was the first time I had heard it mentioned. We still had no idea what was going on except that we were in one Hell of a fight with more German tanks and armor than we had ever seen.

I went to the backdoor to take a last look at that Tiger I had stopped. That big pile of steel was now a raging fire. It always seemed odd to me that something made of steel should burn so well. Of course it wasn't the steel that was burning, but all the gas, oil and grease that burned so easily. The shells and other ammo also added to the blaze. In this case there were five German bodies also burning. As I was gazing into the flames suddenly the fog lifted, the whole landscape turned bright and clear. I could see all the way out to the hills that surrounded Noville. What I saw made my eyes bug out. The forward slope of the hills was covered with enemy tanks and five or six were on the road into town. They had been following the one I helped knock out. Wow! All those tanks out there and me and Joe with only a bazooka.

Those forward tanks had seen that the two dead Tigers had blocked the way into town. When the fog lifted they were in the process of trying to turn around on the narrow road. The next thing that happened was unbelievable, but it happened. Our TDs started firing. First they fired at and destroyed those tanks on the road closer to town. One shot. One tank. They then went after the tanks on the hill. These were swinging around and heading for safety of the reverse side of the hill. Again our Tank Destroyers fired one round after another each hitting dead center on target. I had never seen such shooting. It was like a sharpshooter at an amusement park shooting gallery. I counted twenty tanks blown out of commission in just those few minutes. It was like someone up there was helping those tankers every time they fired. Maybe the Lord was helping a bit. I know he didn't like those Nazi.

I headed back across the street at a trot, ready to speed up if necessary, but the fire from our tankers had quieted the Germans at least for now. By the time I reached the house and went in through the window the fog was back and those hills were once again hidden from view by a great white blanket. The guys had been trying to see what was going on out of the front window but couldn't see very much from that angle. When I came in they turned to ask what had happened, but as they looked at me they stopped and asked, "Good grief, what happened to you. You look like a mess." I discovered that I did look like a mess. I was covered in mud, soot and burns from the rear of the bazooka. My face was a dirty mess also. All of a sudden it hit me. I started shaking and fell down into the chair exhausted. I caught my breath and told them what happened. They liked it all except for the part about no relief just reinforcements. I then went down into the vegetable cellar and fell asleep on the turnips, but I didn't even feel one lump I was so pooped.

WE GET PERMISSION
TO WITHDRAW

I don't know how long I slept, but I felt much better when I woke up and the ringing in my ears and head had almost stopped. It was still there, but I could hear a lot better. I climbed out of the turnip bin and went upstairs. I was asked more questions about what had happened across the street with the big Tiger tank that almost got into town. I told them what had happened again and we discussed the situation. It was after I had thought about all of those tanks, not just the one up front, that I really got the shakes and wondered what the Hell I had been doing out there. I looked out our window and the fog was still there, it fact thicker than ever. We still couldn't see the enemy and he knew right where we were because he had been here before.

I looked out the window and across the street I could make out the shape of the burned out empty Tiger I had knocked out. Under the window was another hulk of a burned German tank, with the remains of a charred body hanging out of the opened hatch. Everywhere I looked there were burned and destroyed vehicles that belonged to us. Most of the houses and building I could see were destroyed. The one we were in was one of the few left that was not totaled. We had a couple of big holes upstairs, but the rest was intact. It looked like pretty soon there would be nothing left here to defend and we would have nothing but rifles to defend it with.

As I looked at two destroyed German tanks I thought of Maxie Slovac. Back in the States, when I was with the machinegun squad of the Third Platoon in C Company, he had been my assistant gunner. He had also been a junk dealer from some place up in New England. When out on maneuvers we often asked him how much could he get for a tank or half-track. He would put on his best Jewish accent and start telling us how many pounds of steel, copper, brass and other stuff there was in the vehicle and how much it was worth per pound as well as its total worth at his junkyard. He would do this with any item we asked about, often adding that he was going to make a fortune after the war. I was transferred to Battalion Headquarters when we got overseas, but my friends from C Company said that they played the same game in combat. Max would grin, put on his accent and rattle off how much a Tiger tank would be worth back home. Maxie had his head about blown off during the Moselle-Saar Valley drive. However I was told that whenever spirits got low someone would holler, "Let's go make junk for Maxie!"

On the 19th of December our team commander asked again if we could withdraw from this crossroad town. He explained we were running out of men, ammunition and equipment. His request was refused. We were again told to hold our position at any cost. Later that day an "88" went right through the barricaded window of the Command Post, killing the commanding officer of the paratroopers and seriously wounding the team leader Major Desobry. The Major was evacuated to a nearby field hospital. The field hospital was over run by the enemy and Major Desobry was a POW for a short time until liberated by our forces some time after Christmas. He recovered and continued his career in the Army, retiring as a Lieutenant General.

Two German Tiger tanks, or what's left of them, sit roadside somewhere outside of Bastogne. I don't know what hit them, but it was sure something more than a bazooka!

The next morning on December 20, I didn't know the date then, a runner came by and said to pack up and get ready to pull out. We were leaving this town to join forces with some paratroopers and some 10th Armored at a place called Foy about ten miles down the road. That is, if we could make it. I had doubts of our having any friendly forces down the road in that direction. Yesterday we had received artillery barrages from that direction. I was outside the house talking to Captain Geiger when the shells came in. At first we thought it was our artillery moving up to give us support, but when the second rounds came in they definitely had the sound of German shells. Even a couple of "Screaming Mimis" passed over. I hoped that our ears had been wrong.

The wounded were loaded into every vehicle that had any room. Until now I had not realized how many had been down the road in the aid station. Orders were passed to destroy anything we couldn't take with us and to blow up any vehicles not running so the Germans couldn't repair and use them. That didn't take us long as we didn't have much left. We had been out of ammo for our tanks and TDs for some time. We were very low on everything else too. While loading up our half-track I noticed there were GIs wearing patches from at least a dozen different outfits. They had joined us as their outfits had been run over by the enemy. We had three soldiers, each from different outfits come over to ride with us.

After the machinegun had been put back in its place on the ring mount, I went back into the house to make a final check to make sure we had everything. I looked around but found nothing but my heavy GI overcoat draped over the back of the big chair. It was heavy and long, but very warm. I decided the best way to transport it was to wear it. I had two bandoleers of M-1 rifle ammo crisscrossed across my chest over my field jacket. I slid out of the ammo belts. Put on the coat and returned the bandoleers back to where they had been. Sarge was hollering at me to get my ass out there so out through the window I went and almost landed on top of him in the half-track. I told him all was clear and the driver put the track in gear and we headed over to take our position in the column.

The fog that had been so helpful to the enemy now became our friend. It was still damp and could, but it hid our withdrawal. It was hard to see what was up ahead. Once we got out of town the road was lined with large trees running along each side. More important was the fact that they had a hard time seeing us. I looked back at the ruined town as it disappeared into the fog. There was nothing left but a pile of rubble. Ours was the only building left standing. Even the church steeple had been blown away. I had been nearby when it came down. The fall killed a tank officer who had stayed up there against orders to try and spot targets for his tanks. I don't see how he could have seen very far with all of this fog, but he thought he could.

The last thing I saw of the town was a battered sign sticking up through a pile of rubble. It proclaimed the town's name was Noville. I remembered that name for in my mind I thought that now it certainly was "no village." The town had been one of the prettiest we had seen in a long time. All of the houses and buildings had been repaired from previous war damage and had been painted. The streets were clean and neat telling of people who cared about their village. Down in the part of France and Germany where we had been fighting there were still places that had not been rebuilt from World War I. I turned around to see what I could see in the thick fog in front of us. Directly ahead of us was a Jeep loaded with wounded and running on its rims. The tires were all but gone with just a few dark shreds of rubber still showing. No time to change tires even if we had them.

Leading the column were two Sherman tanks, then a truck full of infantry from many different divisions, then a Jeep, and then us in our half-track. It was hoped that there was only German infantry between us and the town of Foy and our tanks would scare them off. We hoped also that they didn't know that we had no shells for those tanks. I had talked to one of the guys in the Jeep in front of us as we were loading up. He had been a cook in his division's officer's mess and had never even held a gun before to say nothing of firing one. He had always just been a cook. He added that he was given a rifle in Noville and he learned how to use it damn fast. I hoped so for he was an infantry rifleman now.

It was silent now. No artillery exploding. No machinegun or rifle fire. Only the rumble of our column as we moved slowly along the road and the heavy fog seemed to muffle that. The further we went into the fog the more the tension built wondering where the Germans were and if and when they were going to attack. I was sweating, but not from the temperature as that was around the freezing point. We all had a bad case of the nerves. We could not see very far past the large trees that had been planted along this road maybe a hundred years ago. Over here, that would have been considered rather recent. They must have made a nice shady arch over the road in summer, but their limbs were bare now and looked almost black from wetness.

Suddenly the silence was shattered by a loud blast. The fog up front turned bright orange. The lead tank had been hit and hit hard. There were a couple more blasts then all Hell broke loose. Machinegun and rifle fire hit our column up and down, fired by an enemy well hidden by the fog. One of our two tanks came backing out of the fog at full speed and stopped with a crash as it hit a tree. It had been hit, but was not burning. The other was on fire. We could not see it but we could see the red orange from the flames and hear ammo exploding from the heat. Everybody had his vehicle in reverse. The truck came out of the fog backwards with men jumping out to seek cover in ditches along the road. The Jeep in front of us didn't make it far as it was hit by machinegun fire and rolled over as the wounded tried to escape. I could see some had been killed, but I had to turn my head as our driver had us in reverse too.

We didn't get very far as we plowed into an abandoned truck behind us. Heavy small arms fire was coming out of the fog on our left flank. I grabbed the machinegun and swung it around on its ring mount so it was aimed in the direction that we were receiving enemy fire. I pulled the bolt back to fully load the chamber and was about the answer the enemy's fire. Sarge yelled at me, "Don't fire. You'll give our position away!" I was about to tell him that I thought the son's of bitches damn well knew where we were when a tree burst hit above us. Shrapnel showered down all around, but by some miracle no one was hit. However, a piece had struck the machinegun and now the bolt couldn't be moved. We all bailed out and started to run back toward the rear of our column to regroup with the others, at least with those that were not lying dead in the road.

As I went over the side of the half-track I wondered what had happened to the "Friendly Forces" we were supposed to join here at Foy. Our bluff with our two Sherman tanks had not worked. They had Tigers waiting in the fog. I started to run down the road outside the trees and opposite the side from where all the fire was coming. However, I did not make very good progress for when I crouched down to run low to keep under the stream of bullets, I stepped on the tail of my long overcoat and fell flat on my face in the mushy grass. After hitting the ground a couple times it was clear that the coat had to go. Now this was no simple task. It had to be done flat on my back to avoid being cut in half by the rifle and machinegun fire covering the whole area only about three feet above the ground. I rolled over onto my back. First I had to wriggle out of the bandoleers of ammo for my rifle, then I had to fight my way out of the coat and get the ammo back on. I left the coat there, but I had a feeling that those M-1 bullets might come in handy.

When I was a little further down the road I crawled into a small, very shallow drainage ditch that ran down the road's edge. It was lined with men on their bellies inching their way toward the rear. The ditch didn't really give one much cover, but it made you feel a bit safer. The small arms fire, rifle and machinegun, kept up a deadly pace with no break in the firing and now the artillery was beginning to shell in earnest. I eyeballed the other side of the street. That was a much better place to be. There was ditch and a bank there. One could even sit up. There was no getting over there unless the firing slacked up. A couple of guys had tried and now lay dead on the far edge of the road. I looked at the soles of the boots of the guy in front of me. I couldn't lift myself up high enough without getting hit to see the person behind me. However, we all seemed to slide backward through the mud at the same time. I guess it was some sixth sense that often clicks in during an emergency.

A couple of yards in front of me a medic was working on a soldier with his arm blown away. He had his patient propped up against the trunk of one of the large trees at an angle so that they were shielded from the gunfire. Another round of artillery came in and exploded in the tree above us. When a tree burst occurs the shrapnel covers a wide area like an inverted cone. I cold hear those sharp chunks of steel ripping through the tree limbs as they headed for earth. I instinctively hunched down trying to make myself as small as possible. The shrapnel hit all around me, but none hit me. The medic under the tree was not so lucky. He was hit. Hit hard! He hollered to his fellow medic working the other side of the street, "Hey, Charlie, I'm hit!" He started to run across the road to his buddy, but only made it half way. Blood was gushing out of a big hole clean through his back and chest. He was dead. Later as I crossed the street near his body I looked down at him and when I saw the size of the hole that piece of shrapnel had made I knew I had seen a dead man running.

I started to inch my way back down the little ditch again, but my feet hit the helmet of the guy right behind me. I tapped him lightly on the top of his head with my foot and told him to get going. I did it again, but still no response. I twisted myself and looked around to see what the matter was. He was lying there still and dead. There was no one in the ditch behind him. The others were long gone. When I crawled over him I saw that the shrapnel had hit him too. I also noted that he was the tank officer that had written me up for the Silver Star. A little further down the ditch I came to a place where one of our knocked out trucks would give me some cover to cross the road. I ran across and slid into the ditch in front of me and mushed up against a pile of snow. This was much better. Although the bank and ditch gave no protection from the artillery fire, I was safe, at least for the time being, from all of that small arms fire.

I pushed my back up against the bank and looked at the scene before me. What a mess! Dead were lying all around on the road and in the ditches. Some were hanging out of their vehicles; killed before they could get out and seek cover. Our trucks and half-tracks were either burning or had been torn to shreds by the enemy fire. One quick look was enough. I knew we had to get the Hell out of this place and damn soon before those Jerries came out of the fog after us. I said a little prayer for the dead and myself and wondered if I might be the next to get it.

A Bloody Trail to Bastogne

I looked to my right in the direction of Noville and saw Captain Geiger and another officer. Even at my distance I could hear the Captain cussing, not so much the enemy, but the fact that we had little or nothing to fight back with. I waved at him, but I don't think he saw me as he didn't wave back. A shell hit just a little to my left and I looked to see how close it has come. It had hit too close for comfort, but no damage had been done. I looked back to my right and had planned to join Captain Geiger, but both of the officers were gone. They had disappeared into the fog. I crawled down to where they had been, but could not tell where they or the rest of the troops had gone. I was all alone except for the Germans some place out there in the fog. How long they would stay out there and not come in through the fog I did not know, but I had a feeling it wouldn't be long. I had to get out and find the others.

I knew that the general plan was to fall back and cut across land to Bastogne if we could not join up with forces in Foy. The enemy firing had let up a good bit so I started down the ditch keeping below the top of the bank. I kept looking to see signs in the snow and mud that would give me a trail to follow back to safety. I saw a spot across the road that looked like some had headed out into the fog toward Bastogne. I crossed the road stepping between the bodies of men from my outfit and other outfits that had joined us. I saw tracks in the snow and headed out into a field that looked like a cow pasture. I was only a short distance from the row of trees when I heard a blast and I was blown into the air. I landed flat on my back. My helmet flew in one direction and my rifle went in another.

Our troops move toward the enemy down a Belgium road and out over the countryside. The snow didn't come until December 21st, the day after I was hit, but it was wet and foggy like that with the soldiers on the road.

I was out for a minute or two and when I came to I was numb from the concussion. I looked to my left and almost in reaching distance was the tail of a German mortar shell sticking out of the center of the hole it had blasted in the soft ground of the cow pasture. Thin wisps of blue-gray smoke were still swirling out of the hole. Feeling began to return to my body. I tried moving my arms and legs. They were still a little numb, but everything was working and there was no blood. I started to move and felt something sticking in my back. I reached back and felt a large piece of shrapnel sticking out of the small of my back, less than an inch from my backbone. I could feel it sticking out through my shirt and my field jacket, but there was no blood and it didn't hurt.

All the numbness was gone, just a strange tingling sensation all over my body. I looked over to the smoking mortar shell that was so close and realized I had truly been lucky. Most of the shrapnel had been buried or deflected by the mud. It was time to get the Hell out of this mud hole. Running low I headed for my M-1 that lay just ahead in the direction I thought I should go. I had only taken a few steps when a burp gun chattered in the fog across the street. The bullets tore the field jacket off my back and passed so close to my nose that I could feel the heat from the tracers. The ones that hit me went right through my right leg. Through the shinbone and one just behind that bone in the calf of my leg. This one cut the artery. I could see the path of the bullets as they came out by the trail of blood following them. I fell flat down in the mud again, this time on my face.

Having been hit twice in such a short interval was quite a shock. I was sure my time was up and I would soon be joining my dead comrades that lay all around me. I took a deep breath and said goodbye to Mom and Dad and to my steady girlfriend Joan McDonald. I waited for death to come. I don't know what

I expected, but I waited just the same. Nothing happened. Then, from a place inside of me or outside, I heard a voice say, "You're not dead yet!" I looked down at the leg that had been hit. The pant leg that was still tucked into my combat boot was full of blood and blood was still gushing out on to the grass. It was easy to tell that the artery had been cut, not only by the amount of blood that had poured out, but also by the spurting action of the blood still flowing. I knew I had to do something quick or I really would be dead. There were no medics around to call. In fact, I was all alone on the edge of that foggy field.

I was feeling weak already. I pulled my webbed belt out of my trousers and put it around my leg just above the knee. I pulled it as tight as I could. It slowed the bleeding a good bit, but did not stop it. It stopped it OK when I pulled on it hard, but I couldn't do it for long. I had visions of my passing out and letting the belt go and thus bleeding to death. The vision of a friend who had bled to death after the medic attending him had been killed flashed in my mind. We found them laying side by side, the medic's hand just inches from the tourniquet he was applying. I shook my head to clear it a bit and with my combat knife cut the cloth straps from one of the bandoleers of ammo still around my neck. I inserted the knife under the belt around my leg. This stopped the blood, but I could not get that damn knife tied in the twisted position.

This had worked fine back in the States during "Self Aid" lessons when I could sit up to get at it. Here every time I tried to sit up someone shot at me or shrapnel from a burning tank streaked past. Once, fragments from a mine that exploded came so close that they brush-burned the end of my nose and cut my cheek. There was no sitting up here. I tried and tried to tie that knife in place, but no dice. I would start to pass out and my hand would loosen up and bleeding would start again. Again I had the feeling that I wasn't going to make it. Then from somewhere I got a bright idea. There was a clip of rifle ammo lying on the ground near me. It had fallen out of the bandoleer when I was cutting off the straps. I picked it up with my free hand, the one not holding the knife tight. I pulled the bullets out of the clip with my teeth and then started inserting them under the belt. Each time I slid a bullet under the belt it got a little tighter around my leg. Finally when I had all the bullets from the clip under my belt it pulled the belt tight enough to stop all of the bleeding.

I pulled the knife out and relaxed. I was tired, very tired, but did not feel like I was going to pass out. My body was still numb from the mortar shell blast and my ears were still ringing loudly. I looked back at my leg. It was a bloody mess, but my new tourniquet was still working and I still felt no pain. I knew it would come sooner or later so I looked around to see what my situation was. This didn't give my morale any lift at all. Here I sat in a Belgium cow pasture, fog was all around and I was alone. No one alive anywhere near me. Even the Germans had stopped firing. The silence was unique and ghostly. The crackling of fire from burning vehicles some how only added to the loneliness. All around me were large patches of snow that were feeding the fog like smoke machines. Suddenly I heard a shell coming in. It hit down the road a piece and started issuing large clouds of billowing orange smoke. I knew what that was for. It was to show the more distant artillery where to fire. It didn't bother me. This time I thanked the fog because I knew it was too thick for that signal to show far enough. I was right about that. No artillery came.

Now that the firing had stopped, I crawled over to my rifle. Still no small arms fire so I sat up and checked out my M-1. I brushed the mud off the stock and cleaned it up around the bolt. The bore was clean and there was a full clip of bullets in the magazine. I was ready, but ready for what I didn't know.

But, if the Germans came I would shoot at least one and maybe I could get two. Again, no thoughts of being a hero, it just made sense to me at the time. We had found out they weren't taking many or any prisoners, not even those that could walk. Word had been passed that somewhere not too far from where I was they had lined up and shot over a hundred healthy prisoners. They weren't about to take me with my leg in this condition. I looked around some more. One the road I could see four or five of our knocked out vehicles, some still burning and others silent hulks. I knew there were more in both directions that I couldn't see. It was like a junkyard. That made me think of Maxie and I thought, "There's a lot of junk for you old buddy. Too bad they are all ours." Maybe he heard me up there. Who knows?

I lay there for some time. I don't know how long it was, but it seemed like forever. I had gotten so lonely that I thought even seeing Germans wouldn't be so bad. About that time I heard movement off in the fog in the direction I had intended to run. It got louder and I could hear voices, German voices muttering out there. They were getting closer and heading right toward where I was laying. As I lay there, staring into the fog, I gently slid the bold on my M-1 back to bring my rifle to full load. It made a little noise in spite of my precaution, but they did not hear it. They were so close now I could see the shadowy shape of the point man. I aimed my rifle at him and was waiting for him to get a bit closer before I pulled the trigger, when a large voice back in the fog shouted orders in German. They all turned around and ran back the way they had come. The fog consumed them and I was alone again. That temporary thought about even being glad to see Germans had vanished as soon as I heard them.

A little while later I heard the sound of a vehicle coming down the road. It was the sound of a small vehicle and was coming from the direction of Noville. Once again I was staring into the white wall of fog wondering what was going to happen. I saw it slowly take shape as it neared. It was one of our Jeeps with soldiers in it wearing American uniforms. I was about to yell for help when I remembered we had run across Germans with our equipment and in our uniforms several times. I swallowed the yell and watched them closely. They stopped in the road opposite me and one got out to look at a dead guy in the road. He reached down and did something. Then I saw him remove the dead soldier's dog tags and put them in his pocket. There was nothing German or enemy-like about his actions. I decided to give my yell, but I wasn't sure I had enough strength left to make them hear. I gave it my all. They almost jumped out of their socks. The driver got out of the Jeep and both came running over to me.

I knew the driver. It was Corporal Still. He drove the major's Jeep. The other was a medic from the 101st paratroopers. While Still was explaining to me that they had gotten lost in the fog and had been dodging Germans for a day and a half the medic dumped some of that yellowish powder on my leg wound. He stammered that it was dangerous here and said we should get out. I agreed one hundred percent. They helped me over to the Jeep and helped me into the back. I told Still to turn the vehicle around and head back keeping a sharp lookout for tracks and footprints on our left. We went by the tank that had backed out of the fog and I heard a moan from inside. I told Still to stop. They checked the tank and found him alive in the driver's seat. They got him out and brought him over to the Jeep. He was pretty much out of it, but he did recognize me and said hello. There was a small triangular shaped wound on his forehead. Not messy, but I thought I could see his brain. He was made as comfortable as possible on the hood and we were off again.

I had not felt any pain yet, but I was afraid it might hit me at any moment and interfere with our getting back to safety. I asked the medic if he had any morphine. He said yes and gave me a shot. Shortly after that I saw the tracks pulling off the road and heading across country. There was no mistake this time. It was very obvious that a large group had gone across the soft turf of the field. My first choice has been close, but far enough to get me into trouble. We followed the muddy tracks through the fog. We were afraid that sooner or later we would run into Germans. They had been all over this location, but they were gone now. Still tried to drive as smoothly as possible. Every time we hit a very rutty section or the Jeep slid in the mush, the man on the hood would groan. Once or twice we stopped and the medic checked him. One time he had to push him back on the hood. We had driven so far that we were beginning to think we had gotten lost in spite of following the tracks, when we saw a Jeep up ahead. We slowed down with apprehension, but a friendly voice, an American GI voice hailed us and waved us over to them. It was a medical unit waiting outside Bastogne to help any stragglers. We had reached the safety of our forces at last.

This is Foy, Belgium, the place that we were trying to get to when withdrawing from Noville. From its looks it is hard to figure why one would want to get there.

One was "Doc" Neflen, our Battalion Dental Surgeon and the other medic that I didn't know. Doc checked the man on the hood and he was dead. He died somewhere along the bumpy road in spite of our efforts. He then put a regular tourniquet on my leg. While he was doing this a lieutenant from the 101st came over to ask if any of his Troopers were out there that needed his help. I told him that the only soldiers out there were dead and beyond help. Doc told Still to follow him into town and we pulled up at the Battalion Aid Station and I was put on a stretcher and carried into the building and downstairs to the basement. Down in the basement of the building it was packed with wounded on stretchers. There was not much room left and there was not a great deal of light, but it sure did look good to me. The Battalion Surgeon came over to me and asked what had happened. I pointed to my right leg and said something like this, "It's my right leg again Doc. I think I messed it up pretty good this time." He agreed with me and I passed out. (At the time I wasn't seeing or feeling too good and had just assumed that it was our same battalion surgeon that had been taking care of a bad knee that had developed after a 25-mile hike back in the States. I had to wear an elastic bandage around it even in combat. However, our regular surgeon got sick just before we were ordered to the "Bulge" and this was a new one I had never met.) The rest of this chapter is about what I don't remember, well almost. I came to every once in a while, but most of what now occurs was like a dream.

The first one of these hazy memories was a loud explosion and a wall nearby came crashing down. A bomb had hit the building. I just got a dusting of stone chips and powder with some wood splinters mixed in. Medics lifted me and carried me to another part of the basement. Some patients were not so lucky and were buried under the rubble. In my delirium I had visions of being home, being in a hot tub, and being clean again. I also had fantasies about food, like steak dinners, apple pie and all of those wonderful meals my mother used to serve. In these dreams there was also a pretty young nurse taking care of my needs.

I was out of it all together for a while, no dreams or fantasies. No nothing! Then I began to feel like I was moving. I was in some vehicle riding, riding, riding, and then stopping over and over again. The dreams included Germans and much moving around then riding again. This was all very hazy and made no sense to me at all. I wasn't conscious of what was happening. These things came to mind later like remembering a dream from the night before. One thing I lost during this period of semi-consciousness was a sense of time and night and day. When I finally regained consciousness it was like coming out of a deep sleep. My eyes opened and I saw a neat clean ceiling above me. I looked to my right and there was a guy on a stretcher. The olive drab Army blanket was pulled over his head. There was a yellow Army Quartermaster tag tied to his big toe on his right foot that stuck out from the bottom of the blanket. He was dead. He was Quartermaster material now.

This did not bother me, except I felt sorry for whoever it was. I looked to my left and saw the same thing, another dead guy with a yellow tag. Now this bothered me. Somehow I found the strength to lift my head up to look around the room. It was full of dead men with yellow tags on their big toe. I looked down and sure enough there was a Quartermaster tag on my toe too. I took another look and realized I was in a temporary morgue. Now this shook me up a good bit. I hollered. In a second an Army nurse stuck her head in the door. When she saw me her face turned as white as her uniform. She told me, "Don't move. I'll be right back!" She came right back with a couple of orderlies. They moved me out into the hall and down to the end of a long line of patients waiting on stretchers to see the surgeon.

The nurse checked me out and made some notes on her clipboard. They hung a bottle of plasma over me and once again I had a tube in my arm. They must have decided that I was alive for one of the men in white uniforms removed the Quartermaster tag from my toe. That meant I was no longer Army property, but had been returned to the status of Army personnel.

The line moved slowly, but I finally reached the medical room. The orderlies lifted me onto a table and the doctor took over. Things were beginning to get hazy again and the last thing I remembered was a group of white-clad arms beginning to put a cast on my leg. I blacked out completely and I don't remember a thing until I regained consciousness when a medic was hooking me up to another bottle of that yellowish stuff. I looked around and it seemed like I was in a large tunnel with guys on racks hanging on the walls. I couldn't figure out what the Hell all the noise was about and why this tunnel was swaying back and forth. I felt better and started to get up, but got all tangled up in the tubing I had been hooked up to. The medic came running over and shouted, "Whoa! Where do you think you are going?" My answer was, "I got to get back to my outfit." He laughed and told me to take it easy. I was on a train headed for Paris. I did what he said and to this day I don't know why I said what I said.

I relaxed and looked around and saw that indeed what I thought was a tunnel was a hospital train. My head cleared and there was no more drifting away into another world. I guess it was that blood and other stuff that they had been giving me that brought me back to reality. I can't say I enjoyed the train ride, as it was very rough. The tracks that had been bombed out by our air power earlier in the war had been repaired, but what they needed was rebuilding. Every jolt and bump sent pain all through me. This was in spite of all those little green pills they gave me. My right leg was beginning to throb with pain, but I was alive and heading for a big hospital for treatment. I was laying there thinking of pleasant things like my girlfriend Joan and Mom's good cooking, it took my mind off the pain, when the train ground to a halt a voice from up in the front of the car announce that we had arrived in Paris.

In came the men with stretchers. I was loaded onto one and my bottles of blood came with me, hanging from a stainless steel rod attached to the stretcher. Out of the train car we went and down to the end of the platform where there was a large group of wounded laying in rows waiting for ambulances to come for the trip to the hospital. It was snowing and cold. The snow swirled down in big flakes with most of them melting as they hit the ground. The high roof over the platform kept most of the snow away from us, but occasionally a group of flakes would be blown in under the roof. They looked big and white against the brown of the Army blanket that covered me. The station platform was a very busy place with people and baggage carts going back and forth. A man standing in front of our group announced that the ambulances would soon be here to take us to a hospital. He spoke with a strong French accent and I didn't get the name of the hospital. A lady with a French Red Cross uniform came over to me. She was carrying a paper cup with hot coffee in it. She asked me if I wanted a cup and I said yes. She helped me sit up enough to drink it. I took my first sip and was disappointed. It was nice and hot, but I like my coffee black and this had cream and sugar in it. It turned me off, but I drank half of it and told her that was enough. I could never drink coffee out of a paper cup after that, even black coffee.

It was a nice thing for those ladies to do for us on a cold snowy day and I'm sure most of the patients enjoyed it very much. The ambulances backing up to the loading dock interrupted my thoughts about the coffee. It was snowing harder now and the streets were getting slushy. I was guided into the back of the ambulance with others. The driver and his assistant were standing by the back doors of the vehicle waiting to close them once we were in. The driver was a Frenchman and his assistant a French lady. They were both very old, so old that they looked like they should have been rocking in some home for the aged, not standing out in this cold snowy weather. They were both small and thin and I guess that made them look even older. They shut the doors and secured them, then got in the front. As the driver tried to pull away I could feel the rear wheels spinning in the mushy snow. The rear end of the ambulance fish-tailed back and forth a few times and then we were off heading down a busy Paris street.

I couldn't see what was happening out there, but I sure could feel the ambulance sliding all over the place. I could hear the little old man up front cussing at the traffic. He was speaking French, but cussing sounds the same in any language even if you don't know the words. I recognized a few words that my French-Swiss grandfather used when something went wrong. I wonder how the little old driver was going to handle this vehicle on these slippery streets. It was a wild ride, but that guy did a great job and we arrived at the hospital safely. I heard later that one load of patients had not been so lucky. Their driver had lost control of his vehicle and it had crashed into traffic and rolled over. When I heard that I wished that there was some way I could have thanked the couple for the great job they did, but I didn't even know his first name. The driver pulled his vehicle up to an entrance marked "Ambulance" at the side of a large red brick building that had been a French civilian hospital before the U.S. Army took it over after the liberation of Paris. Two hospital attendants came out rolling a gurney and slid me on to it.

I was rolled into the building and down a long corridor. I looked up and saw silver tinsel and many different colored Christmas balls hanging down from the ceiling. As we turned a corner there was a large cardboard Santa smiling at me. I had forgotten all about it being December and Christmas coming. It seemed years since I had hung that sprig of evergreen on the front of the half-track. One looses track of time, except for day and night, when in combat. The mind becomes consumed with the enemy and trying to stay alive. My mind was free of those thoughts now. The enemy was far away and someone else had the responsibility to keep me alive. I now felt sure I was going to make it.

I wondered what day it was and was about to ask my pusher when we arrived at the side of a real hospital bed with snow-white sheets. These were the first sheets I had seen since I had left home. They lifted me on to the bed and a nurse came and hooked me up to another bottle of fluid. When she finished with the bottle she asked me if I was hungry. I suddenly realized that I was. It had been a long time since I had eaten any real food. I told her yes and in a very short time she returned with a tray of hot food with a full set of utensils for eating. I don't remember what the meal was, only that it sure tasted good and made me feel great.

I had just finished eating when the nurse came back. This time there was a doctor with her. They stopped at the foot of my bed and started looking at my medical record that was hanging there. After some head nodding and mumbling the doctor came over and asked me how I felt. I told him that I felt better than I had felt for a long time. He went to the bottom of the bed and a ward boy pulled the covers back and removed a wire cage that had kept the blankets from weighing on my bad leg. I was still sitting up from eating my dinner and I looked down and I saw my leg in a cast for the first time. It didn't look good. My toes sticking out of the end had turned a nasty looking greenish black and there were yellowish brown stains all over the once white plaster cast.

The doctor lifted up the cast. He tried to be gentle, but it hurt like Hell, so bad it almost turned my stomach. As he lifted it up the whole bottom of the cast fell away. A soggy brown mess, and what a stink! The smell hit me like the odor from a hundred dead rats that had been out in the hot sun all day. I knew that smell. It came from the dead flesh of my leg. I had gangrene. My leg was eased down and the doctor came over to me with a worried look on his face. He was trying to tell me something but couldn't find the words. I said, "Gangrene?" The worried look left and he answered yes. Before he could say anything else, I responded with, "I guess it will have to come off." He said yes, he would have to amputate it the first thing in the morning. He said he was sorry to have to make such an operation on Christmas day, but the gangrene was spreading and the leg had to be removed as soon as possible. I now knew what day or night it was. It was Christmas Eve, 1944.

He apologized again and said he would send the chaplain to see me and he was gone to see other patients on his ward. It didn't take long for the chaplain to come. We talked a bit and we said a prayer together and then he left. He could see my morale was OK. It's no fun losing a leg on any day, but one look or smell told me it was no good. I guess my spirits were up for a couple of reasons. One, I had almost died on that Belgium pasture and had even come to in a morgue. Now I was safe and was going to live. I thanked God that he had been with me and helped me to safety and back into his wonderful world.

The nurse came back and gave me a shot and a pill. I think the shot was morphine. I don't know what the pill was. The pain in my leg had gotten very bad. It was a rotten sick kind of pain, one that was very depressing. The shot and/or the pill kicked in and I went to sleep in spite of the pain. When I woke up it was morning and two ward boys were there with the "meat wagon," more correctly called a gurney. They lifted me on to it and off we went to the operation room. When we arrived it the "prep-room" a man in white came over to me holding a device that looked like a large mouthed bolt cutter. He started to cut the cast off my leg. I suddenly had the desire to take one last look at it even though I knew it wouldn't be a pleasant sight. I asked the guy with the cutters if he minded if I watched him. He said, "Hell no. If you don't mind, why should I?" I was watching him cut down the side of the cast when nurse walked over. She was holding a big-ass needle. She said, "Count to ten," and stuck the needle in my arm. I remember getting to eight, then nothing more. I never did get to see my leg.

When I came out from underneath the anesthetic I was in a small room and I heard Christmas music drifting in from the hallway. An Army nurse was standing over me. She had just removed a thermometer from my mouth and was giving it a good look. I was hot. I was burning up. She looked at me and said, "Merry Christmas." As she made some notes on her clipboard, I asked her, "I guess it is still pretty high?" She replied no that it was almost back to normal. I asked her how come I was so hot. She checked my bed and then laughed. I asked her what was so funny. She didn't answer, but started taking blankets off my bed. I counted seven that she removed. These plus the one she left on the bed made a total of eight blankets that had been on me.

Then I laughed too. I had no way of knowing that this had been the cause of my sweating as there was a wire cage over the lower section of my body that kept the weight of the blankets off the operation. It seems that on the way back from the operating room I had to be rolled across an open courtyard in the center of the hospital building. It was cold and still snowing. Someone made sure that I wouldn't get a chill or possibly worse. The nurse went away with the blankets and I soon cooled down. I felt pretty good. My head was clear and there was no pain. In fact I couldn't even tell that my leg was gone. I could still feel it down there like I still had it. The nurse was back again. This time she asked me if I would like a drink. Thinking she meant water, I said no. She answered by saying that she meant a drink to celebrate Christmas. I said yes to this. I had a choice and I chose scotch and water. I had two because I was a special patient. She explained that the officers at the hospital had saved their liquor ration for the patients to celebrate on Christmas day.

That's how I celebrated Christmas in 1944, with two drinks of scotch, a pretty nurse and Christmas carols in the background, all of this in the great city of Paris, France. For a while the war seemed like a bad dream in the distant past. I thanked my nurse and told her to be sure and thank the other officers who had given up their drinking time for the patients in that French hospital. Later the chaplain came by again to see how I was making it. We had a nice chat and he helped me to thank God that I was here to celebrate another Christmas.

The spell after my operation in which I did not feel any pain did not last very long. The pain from the amputation was terrible and those pain pills and shots did little to curb it. It was a severe tingling type of pain that started in my stump and then ran through my entire body. It was a nerve pain much like a very bad electric shock. They told me it would get better as the skin grew back over the end of my stump and protected those raw nerve endings. Static from the intercom or a radio had the effect of a cattle prod, even of torture. They finally disconnected the buzzer and loudspeaker in this small recovery room.

This did not put anyone in jeopardy, as there was usually a nurse or medic in the room anyhow. There were two double amputees in beds nearby and their suffering was so great that they moaned and hollered most of the time. I really felt sorry for them and was glad that I only had one stump to hurt. The guy in the bed next to me said not to feel too sorry for them. They had been shot while stealing rations and supplies from a train that was headed for the front lines. Now I knew why sometimes when we opened K-Rations there were no cigarettes, coffee, sugar or other goodies that were supposed to be there for us. These guys had stolen them. They stripped the stuff that brought big money on the Black Market, resealed them and put them back. This time they were caught. Their moaning was still unpleasant, but I know longer felt so sorry for them.

I was moved out of the recovery room the next day and into a regular orthopedic ward. The ward was so full I don't think they could have squeezed another bed into it. The vast majority had been wounded during the Battle of the Bulge. (It didn't get that name until later.) My pain was less and somehow, because I knew it was a "getting better" pain it was easier to tolerate. The pain before the operation had been a sick pain caused by the gangrene. It was the pain of a dying part of my body and would only get worse and could lead to my death. The regular hot meals and the warm dry surroundings of the hospital also helped me to feel better each day. I was sitting up in bed and enjoying my surroundings.

One of these enjoyments was a visit from a young pretty French nurses aide. I dug back into my mind and found a bit of the French I had learned around home and in classes at high school and at George Washington University in D.C. I had gotten in a semester of college before I was called to active duty. We were getting along fine, language wise that is. She brought me a red and white-checkered ditty bad that the ladies of the French Red Cross had made for the patients. It was filled with interesting and helpful things for a patient that had lost all of his personal belongings. At each visit my French got better and she got friendlier. I had thoughts of dates in Paris with her showing me the town and maybe even falling in love. However, our friendship was short lived as on or about December 30 I left the hospital and was headed to England. There they said I was to get an airplane ride back to the States.

I'm in England
But Never See It

It was another ambulance ride to the train station, but this time no snow, just cold, very cold weather. The train took us to the waterfront in a large city. I think it was Cherbourg. German POWs still in their Nazi uniforms unloaded us. They carried my stretcher over to a small fishing type boat where they stopped with a click of their heels. They stood by the narrow gangplank at attention with me between them. Their uniforms looked almost new and they were all spit and polish. They stared straight ahead with faces like stone, showing no expression at all. The wind had gotten very cold. I was warm under my blankets, but could feel the icy blast on my face. The two stretcher-bearers stood like statues facing the cold. After about fifteen minutes of being held like this I began to worry that they might get tired and drop me. I tried to tell them that it was OK with me if they set me down and took a break, but they gave no indication that they even heard me. Most of the German soldiers we had captured understood and spoke English. It was part of their training for when they conquered America.

I figured that these guys just chose to ignore me. I even wondered what they would do if I suddenly hollered out, "Hiel Hitler!" I decided that would not be a very wise move on my part, so I just waited with them hoping they were as strong as they looked. I sure hoped that we didn't use POWs as stretcher-bearers up near the front. It would have been quite a shock if I had seen these two Germans holding me the first time I came to. I would have thought that I'd been captured. Finally another

German came over and said something to them in German and they came alive. They carried me up the narrow gangplank that belonged to the boat that we had been standing in front of. That plank swayed and wobbled something awful, but the Germans kept their footing and soon I was being lowered into a square hole in the deck.

Now that I was aboard the boat it looked smaller than ever. It was, or had been, a commercial fishing craft. It still had the large booms, but now they held no nets. The boat was very clean, probably a lot cleaner than it had ever been in its fishing days. When I arrived at the hatch, I had learned that was what they called this square hole in the deck, I looked over the edge of my stretcher and saw a ladder going straight down into the belly of the ship. In order to get me down there my stretcher had to be tilted almost vertical. I felt like I was going to slide off any second and plunge down there all by myself. However, we made it down OK. I still don't know what kept me on that stretcher.

The hold of the boat was filled with hospital beds with their side rails up. It was a small ship all right, but there were a lot of patients squeezed in down below. It was nice and comfy once I got settled in. I remembered the Army transport that had brought me across the Atlantic and into Cherbourg harbor in September. The ship had to drop anchor quite a way out of the harbor due to obstructions in the water caused by our bombing. We made the trip to the dockside on large self-propelled barges. I guess this was one of the reasons they were using these small fishing vessels to carry us across the English Channel to the British Isles.

The crew that was taking care of the patients stowed where once fish were hauled were old British men and women. I don't know who was sailing the ship as I never saw any of them. It was nice and quiet lying there in the neat white bed with the sides pulled up. There were the gentle lapping sounds of waves against the wooden hull. When we got under way it was a different story. The English Channel was quite rough and the small boat did a lot of rocking from side to side and pitching up and down. It was a bit scary at first, but after a bit I got used to it. The nice English people around me helped me feel secure. It was obvious that they had made this crossing many times before.

A smiling gray-haired lady who handed me a plate full of bacon and eggs interrupted my thoughts. They were fried eggs sunny side up. What a surprise. I hadn't seen fried eggs for some time. Even back in the garrison at Camp Gordon, Ga., we seldom, if ever, got fried eggs. They sure looked pretty and the coffee that came with them smelled good too. I thanked the lady and I thanked the Lord that the rough ride had not made me the least bit seasick. I concluded that I would have made a good sailor. The eggs would have tasted better with a little salt and pepper on them, but they were enjoyed very much anyhow. I later learned that the British use little or no seasoning on their cooking.

I must have fallen asleep for the next thing I knew there was a lot of people moving around in a hurry and someone was shouting, "All ashore for Southampton." The boat had stopped and I could no longer hear the engine running. Getting out of the hold was like my arrival only in reverse. This time I went straight up and those carrying me were English civilians. I was surprised to look out and see that it was night. I had lost track of time again. I went down the wobbly gangplank and over to a nearby hospital train. It was British, but so was everything else. I was in England. When the train had been loaded and we were traveling off into the black of night, a very British voice came over a loudspeaker and announced that we were headed for Oxford. Most of my life I had heard of Oxford, England, and the University and now I was going there.

WESTERN UNION

1201

A. N. WILLIAMS
PRESIDENT

The filing time shown in the date line on telegrams and day letters is STANDARD TIME at point of origin. Time of receipt is STANDARD TIME at point of destination

(48)

WS54 31 GOVT=WUX WASHINGTON DC 18 1237P

1945 JAN 18 AM 12 50

MRS R GENEVIVE ADDOR=

1428 GERANIUM ST NORTHWEST=

REGRET TO INFORM YOU YOUR SON PRIVATE FIRST CLASS DONALD J

ADDOR WAS SLIGHTLY WOUNDED IN ACTION TWENTY DECEMBER IN

BELGIUM YOU WILL BE ADVISED AS REPORTS OF CONDITION ARE

RECEIVED=

DUNLOP ACTING THE ADJUTANT GENERAL.

*This is the official notification to my family that I
had been wounded. I'm glad my letter arrived first.*

From one end of the train car came a couple pushing a cart. They were wearing brightly colored paper hats and had crêpe paper garlands around their necks. They were passing out hats, noisemakers and confetti to all the patients. It was then that I realized that it was New Year's Eve. The train rumbled on and in a few minutes a voice came over the loudspeaker announcing that it was five minutes to midnight. The voice then started a countdown. We all joined in and when we got down to zero everyone hollered, "Happy New Year!" We blew our horns and rattled our noisemakers. The car was filled with confetti as strains of "Auld Lang Syne" filled the car. That's how I celebrated the coming year of 1945. A hush then fell over us and all was silent for a while as each of us thought of home and of our buddies who were still fighting the war.

I don't remember how I got from the train to the hospital. The hospital was a "temporary" U.S. Army hospital that had been built on a golf course just outside of Oxford, England. The wards were large Quonset huts. A Quonset hut is a large prefabricated semi-circular building made out of sheets of corrugated steel for their outside skin. They gave the appearance of huge metal pipes with the bottom half in the ground. They were placed in rows and one had to go outside to get from one to the other. Each building held about forty patients. There was one nurse for every two huts, or wards, and one corpsman for each ward. They were heated by two coal burning pot-bellied stoves, one at each end of the building. If you were near a stove you were too hot, while if a little further away you were too cold.

The newer or sicker patients usually got the warm spots. Others depended on blankets to keep them warm. It was nighttime when I arrived on the ward and all was quiet. In the morning I woke with a nurse taking my temperature. Seemed like every time I came out of sleep, a nurse was there taking my temperature, but this was SOP (standard operating procedure) on all wards for all patients. I had the ward boy crank my bed up so I could look around and size up my new surroundings. The rows of beds on each side of the ward were full. Not an empty bed in the place. Some I could see at a glance were a Hell of a lot worse off than I was. After breakfast a couple of the "walking wounded" as they were called at the Battalion Aid Station at the front, came over to see me.

After they said hello and introduced themselves they told me that they had been wounded in the "Battle of the Bulge." They said almost everyone else on the ward had been wounded in this battle too. This was the first time I heard of such as thing as the "Battle of the Bulge." I soon began to realize what a big damn battle it was and my part was just a small bit of the terrible fighting. They asked me what outfit I was in and I told them the 20th Armored Infantry Battalion of the 10th Armored Division. They looked at me with surprise written all over their faces. They asked me where and when I had been wounded. I told them I thought it was the 20th of December when I got hit and we were trying to withdraw from Noville to Foy. They said that couldn't be. Those places were just outside of Bastogne and Bastogne was completely surrounded by heavy German forces. I said I know I was fighting in Noville for about three days and explained how I had seen a sign with Noville sticking up out of the rubble that had once been a pretty little town.

One of the guys went back to his bed to get a map. At the mention of Bastogne it seemed that every patient that could move about had gathered at my bed. They put the map on the edge of the bed and the guy pointed to Bastogne and the long dark line that bulged all around it. He said that was the German front line all around the city by many miles. I looked at the map and saw both Noville and the road that led to Foy and back into Bastogne. I showed them were I was, even where I had been wounded. That was the first time that I heard the name of the town we had been defending "at any cost." They asked how I got out of Bastogne. I told them I didn't know because I passed out in the aid station and didn't come to until a couple of days later when I woke up in a temporary morgue. I didn't know and no one else could tell me how I got out of Bastogne until I met a gentleman while on vacation in Mexico in 1948. (See addendum for this strange meeting.)

The nurse came and chased the guys away. She was there to help give me a sponge bath. I had been cleaned up a bit, particularly where it counted for my operation. I still had the grime from not having a bath for over a month on most of my body. It had also been a long time since I had shaved or been shaved at least on my face. When you were in an outfit "spearheading" a drive for General Patton you didn't have time for such things. You just learned to live with it, the living being the most important part. She gave me a warm soapy washrag and together we made big improvements. It sure did feel good being clean again. The nurse then started on my hands and arms. They were black all the way up to my elbows. I mean they were a real black, almost like dark grease. She was scrubbing me hard enough to feel like she was going to rub my skin away, but it only removed the surface dirt. The black remained. Suddenly I realized what the black was and I knew it couldn't be washed away. Only time and the shedding of skin would do it. The nurse looked puzzled until I told her that the black was blood, my blood that had soaked into my hands and arms when I was trying to stop the bleeding in that Belgium cow pasture.

Not too long after my scrub up the doctor came by on his morning rounds. The doctor said hello and introduced himself, but I don't remember his name. He looked at my chart and them went about changing the dressing on the end of my stump. He told the nurse to have a look and then said to her, "Doesn't that look good!" It looked terrible to me, but I'm no doctor. I found out later that it looked good to them because there was no sign of the gangrene or any other infection. Also, my stump was doing a good job of healing. The dressing changing was a very painful experience particularly when the dressing stuck to the wound. It was all of those recently cut nerve ending that made the hurt so bad.

After the dressing change I got something new, at least new to me. They spread some kind of adhesive on my stump and slipped a hollow tube of cloth over it. The glue was to hold the stockingette to my skin. The end of this thing extended well beyond my stump. Next came a rope with a white canvas bag tied to it. In the bag they placed weights and hung it off the foot of the bed. The doctor explained this contraption was de-signed to help pull the skin down over the end of my stump as it healed. It did a good job of pulling my skin, but it also pulled the rest of me toward the bottom of the bed. This added to the difficulty of sleeping at night.

As the days went by I kept feeling better and looking bet-ter too. The blood stains on my hands and arms were gone and I had put on some of the weight I had lost while in combat, even the pain was much less. I was tired of being confined to this bed and wanted to get out and move about. Most of all I wanted to get out and go to the bathroom. I never did like "ducks" and "bedpans" and now I was sick and tired of them. However, every time I even tried to sit all the way up that wound in my back that had been caused by that mortar shell blast felt like it was splitting open and this hurt. I couldn't remember anyone ever having looked at it since I had arrived in England. I was wondering why?

I had decided that I had better ask the doctor about it when he made his morning rounds the next day. However, the doc beat me to the punch. After checking out my stump, he told me everything down there looked great. In fact, my stump was almost healed over. Then he asked me how come I had not gotten out of bed. When I told him about my back he got an amazed look on his face and said, "What hole in your back?" I told him about the shell fragment that had knocked me down and this sent him back to my chart on the end of my bed. It took some time as my medical file had gotten quite thick and he read every page very carefully. Finally when almost to the last page on that clipboard, he uttered an, "Ah, ha!"

He came over to me and apologized. He told me to turn over and then up came my pajama top. The doctor peeled off the old dressing and cleaned it with some liquid that felt cool. He asked someone for tweezers and I could feel him pulling an object out of my back. I thought it was the piece of shrapnel. I had heard that sometimes they did not remove metal objects from the body during the first operation. That is if it was not the corrosive kind and the wound was a clean one. I could just feel that piece of shrapnel being pulled out of my back. Boy! What a great souvenir. I asked the doc if I could have it. He said sure and handed me a lump of wax. It had been inserted into the wound to make sure the hole drained and healed from the inside out.

He told me to lie still and he went over to his medical cart and came back with a little bottle. He told me he was going to cauterize it and it might hurt a bit. I felt something wet and cool on my back and then Wow! If he hadn't told two good-sized orderlies to hold me down just before the pain came I know I would have gone right up through the roof. The good part was that the pain was very short and was soon gone. All that was left was some sweat on my brow. I asked him what the Hell it was and he told me magnesium. It had literally fried my hide. As the doctor left he said to take it easy for the rest of the day and tomorrow I should be able to sit up OK.

The next day not only was I able to sit up, but I was also able to get up. Oh boy! That meant no more bedpans and "ducks." Going to the bathroom either way was very painful. Taking a crap was the worst and it took longer. I could feel the pain through every nerve in my body, but at least now I would not have to suffer the discomforts of the bedpan.

The first thing I wanted to do after the aforementioned bodily functions was to shampoo my hair. Several months had gone by during which I had not had a chance to take a bath or shower. The Army brought portable shower tents up to the front whenever they could catch up with us. That wasn't often as General Patton kept us chasing those Germans at top speed. Often after capturing our designated objectives for the day or week we would try to take a break for routine maintenance on our tools of war, but Patton would send down word to get cracking after those sons of bitches. He had announced to the press that we had already taken the next two towns. In addition, I had been out on patrol guiding an ammo truck to Company B's positions and had missed the last shower visit. The hospital people had done the best they could while I was in bed, but there is only so much you can do with a washbasin and cloth. Also, there were forty or more other patients on the ward who were a lot worse off than I was and they kept arriving every day. Most were still casualties from the "Battle of the Bulge."

I had been able to get the use of one of the ward's two sets of crutches and had made it into the long row of sinks that ran down the wall on one side of the latrine. It wasn't easy, as this was the first time I had been "on my feet" since I had been wounded on the 20th of December. However, by the time I had made it from my bed half way down the ward to the latrine I had gotten the feel of the crutches and I was pleasantly surprised at how much strength had come back to me. I wondered if I could get through the shampoo while standing on one leg. I couldn't depend on the crutches, as I needed both hands for this job. I thought of calling for help or a chair, but decided to see how I could do on my own. I didn't need any help. The shampooing went fine. I had forgotten to ask for shampoo so I used the brown GI soap that was in the soap dish. It wasn't very sudsy, but it sure did clean my hair and scalp.

As I headed back to my bed I got even more accustomed to walking on crutches. I had never used crutches before and was pleased with the ease I got around on this first trip about as a one legged man. I didn't know anything about artificial legs. I had never even seen one, but I thought getting about on crutches was pretty good. I could make my way through life on these if I had to. I also realized that I had stood there in the latrine on one leg for at least twenty minutes and never once lost my balance, not even one waiver. It seemed that my sense of balance had shifted entirely over to my left leg. This shift of balance has remained with me my entire life. I later had a friend that lost his right hand and he had been right handed. He told me that right from the start his left hand worked just as well as his right had before the loss. He also added that he had not been able to do a lot with his left hand before.

When I got back to my bed it suddenly looked very good to me. My stump was beginning to throb with pain from being in a vertical position for the first time and I was tired, but happy. It felt good to get that traction bag hooked up again. When the nurse came back from tending to patients in the next building she scolded me for taking off on my own for the first time out of bed, but I could tell that underneath the scolding she was pleased with my recovery progress. She had a total of about eighty patients in two different buildings to tend to and now I was one who didn't need close attention.

One of the first things I did when I arrived at the hospital in England was to write home to Mom and Dad. I got a "V-mail" form from the Red Cross lady and wrote a brief note telling them that I had been wounded. I added that I was now in an Army hospital in England and doing fine and that I would be coming home soon. I did not tell them that I had lost my leg. I was worried about how it would affect Mother and I knew her main worry would be about me. I also knew that when they saw me and saw how well I was doing they would feel a lot better. I could also tell them the whole story and they would realize, like I did, that I was lucky to be here at all. From the hospital in Oxford I was not allowed to tell any details about where I had been or what I had been doing. When I had written from the Front I couldn't even mention the weather. It had been raining most everyday since my outfit had landed in France. I remember once when they told me I couldn't mention the weather, I told the OD, "Hell, don't you think the Germans know by now that it is raining!" They were only a few miles away, but the orders from the censors had to be followed or they would block it out anyhow.

The "V-mail" system was the quickest way to get a message home. You wrote your message on a one-page form. The form was then photographed and along with a lot of other letters on that roll of film, it was flown to the U.S. When it arrived the film was developed and printed and your message continued by Stateside mail. It looked funny as it was a negative print looking like white ink on black paper, but it worked. I was hoping my letter would reach home on Geranium Street in N.W. Washington, D.C., before the official government telegram informed my family that I had been wounded and was in this hospital in England. This would ease the shock a bit. It worked. They got my letter before the telegram arrived. I guess due to the large amount of us wounded in the "Bulge" caused an overload, because my "V-mail" form had not been photographed, but arrived just as I had written it. My mother was so nervous when she saw the return address was from the hospital overseas that she ripped it almost in half in her haste to get it open.

Our daytime nurse was a wonderful person and a very good Army nurse. In spite of the fact that she had two large Quonset huts full of wounded soldiers to take care of she always had a beautiful smile on her face and a cheerful word or two for each of her patients. She had reddish blonde hair and a touch of freckles on her face. She was no glamour girl, but a very nice looking lady and to us she was a beauty. There wasn't one of us who didn't dream of taking her into Oxford on a date. I don't know what her name or rank was. She went by the nickname "Swanee." Just her presence on the ward made life, once again, worth living and she reminded us of the girl waiting back home.

The night nurse who came on duty at bout 4 pm was also a nice looking young lady. However, she had absolutely no understanding of the combat wounded men she was attending. She tried hard to understand, but could not comprehend the fact that for an infantryman on the Front, three hours a night had become a good night's sleep. This meant that when we could no longer sleep the usual eight hours in our nice comfy hospital beds and had to get up and do something, we were close to being well. It did not mean we needed sleeping pills! It meant we were getting our bodies and mind ready for that lifestyle back in combat, even though most of us were missing an arm or leg and would never see our old outfit again. She would get upset and her feelings hurt when any of us refused the nightly servings of "Yellow-jackets and Green-hornets." One was a sleeping pill and the other a pain pill. I don't remember which was which.

When I first arrived on the ward this nightly duo of colorful pills was most welcome and played an important in my recovery. I remember the first night I refused them. I felt that I had recovered enough that I could go without this help. I was anxious to get away from as much drugs and medicine as was possible. It was a good feeling to know that you no longer needed the "Yellow-jackets and Green hornets." Those of us who had progressed this far would get up after a snooze and gather at the end of the ward sitting in a circle of chairs smoking and chatting in low voices so as not to disturb those sleeping. We also kept our eyes and ears on new arrivals in case they might need help. We would alert the ward boy or nurse at any indication that a patient might need attention.

I tried to explain all of this to the night nurse, but she could only see "The Book," and the book said the patients should have a full night's sleep and sleeping and pain pills were to be given to make the patients sleep. In the infantry we would have called this doing things by the numbers, but we discovered that "By the Numbers" didn't always apply. It was meant to be a guideline only. One night when she came back on to our ward after checking out the others, she found us sitting in our little group smoking and talking. She immediately started to scold us and ordered us to get back into bed and go to sleep. I tried to explain to her again that we did not want or need sleep and we were not disturbing anyone. It was an extremely cold night and I pointed out to her that we had kept the coal fires burning in both stoves. Some of the guys mumbled thoughts I hoped she didn't hear. She left in a huff slamming the ward door behind her on the way out.

When the door slammed the guys started talking about her and were joined by some in their beds who had been awakened by her outburst. Army talk between Army guys is not so sweet, and is full of very colorful expressions. These guys were no exception and combat had perhaps made the talk rougher. What they said about her was not nice. They were "pissed off!" about her attitude and were saying so in no uncertain terms. Suddenly the lights flashed on and there she stood by the switch plate. She had only pretended to leave the ward and she had heard every word. Well, she had gotten an earful and now she burst out crying. She wailed that she had tried so hard. She wailed this over and over until she was hysterical. The ward boy came and led her out of the ward. We never saw her again.

Most of the guys shrugged it off saying, "Well she asked for it." In a way she sure did, but I still felt sorry for her. As she stood down there at the other end of the ward with tears streaming down her face I suddenly saw a very young girl, one who was homesick and lonely. This was probably her first time so far away from home. It's odd, but many of us on that ward were young and away from home for the first time too. However, combat makes one feel a lot older for his age. I still wouldn't be twenty years old until July and that was four months away. Yet four months in combat and the experience of being wounded made me feel a lot older. So much happened in such a short time that the age you were was not the age you felt. She was a good nurse and knew her nursing, but had not lived enough to be an Army nurse so close to combat. I hoped that the Army would transfer her to a dependents ward somewhere back in the States.

One day when I came back from the clinic I found that there was a new patient in the bed next to mine. He was sitting up in bed and there was a big round bandage on his right foot all the way up to his ankle. We said hello and he introduced himself as Jim Costolonis from Orange, N.J. He was a bit older than I was and the premature hair thinning up front made him look older than he was. After we talked a while I nodded my head toward his bandaged foot and asked him what had happened. Jim said it happened while he was trying to get to sleep in a slit trench he had just dug. He said he tried every position he could think of to get comfortable, but couldn't find one. Now one doesn't have many choices of positions in a slit trench. After about a half an hour of feeling uneasy he got out of the trench and reversed his position. He had just closed his eyes and was falling asleep when a shell hit right next to his hole. A piece of shrapnel flew into the hole and almost severed the front part of his foot from the back. If he had not changed his position just moments before, he would have been hit in the head and killed.

Jim was very nervous and although he thanked our Lord that he had moved and was still alive, he worried about his foot and what it would look like and how he would walk on half a foot. I asked him what it looked like and he said he didn't know he had been afraid to look at it; afraid of what he might see. The next day when the doctor came to change dressings Jim asked me if I would watch and tell him what his foot looked like and what was missing. His foot was not a pretty sight. His toes were shattered and pieced of bone were sticking out. Also, some of the toes had turned black. I had seen toes that color sticking out from my cast and I knew that it was the beginning of gangrene. The back half of his foot and ankle look pretty good, at least from what I could see. The doctor put a new dressing on and told Jim he would have to operate on it early the next morning.

His bed was empty when I woke up. I never did sleep very late, but surgeons really like to start work early and it takes time to prep the patient. It was a little before noon when they brought him back on the "meat wagon." Two strong orderlies lifted him into his bed and the nurse tucked him in making sure he was comfortable. He was still out of it and had a peaceful smile on his face. I hoped he was dreaming of good things at home in New Jersey. It looked like he was. When he came to later on I asked him how he felt. He said his head was a little groggy, but he felt fine. No, his foot didn't hurt and it felt like it was still there. There was one of those "bird cages" over it to keep pressure from the covers off. I asked him what he had been dreaming about. He said he didn't remember dreaming about anything. I told him about the smile that was on his face when they brought him in and he smiled again.

The next day, when they changed the bandages, a different and strange looking foot came into view. The end of it was round and looked like a baseball. Even the surgical stitches looked like those on a baseball. All of Jim's toes were gone, bones and all. The two flaps of skin and flesh that had been left were sewn together in a ball like shape. It was clean and neat but didn't look like anything you could walk on. I saw the worried look come back on Jim's face and I knew he was thinking the same thing. Even when one knows he has been very lucky and is a lot better off than many others around him one worries about his personal problem in dealing with what ever is left after surgery.

Time went by and Jim's foot looked a lot less like a baseball, but it was still quite large where the toes had been. One day during the morning rounds the doctor said that it had healed well enough for Jim to try to bear weight on it. His last words to Jim were to "Try and stand on it." It took a while for Jim to get the nerve to try his funny looking foot on the floor. He slid his legs off the bed and let them hang down. He stared at that thing that had been his foot. I could see by his expression that he was afraid, afraid he would fall on his face. I gave him some encouraging words and he put his good foot on the floor and stood on it. His funny foot was down there too, but he hesitated for a few seconds then shifted his weight on to it.

I didn't have to ask him how it was. Instantly a smile broke out on his face so big and great that it almost swallowed his ears. There was also a big sigh of relief! He put his weight on it and took a little hobble-like step. Then he was back in bed telling about how there was no pain or problem. He knew he would be able to walk on his new foot.

The next time out of bed he walked up the line of beds keeping close to something he could grab if he felt like he was going down. At first it was a wobbly walk, but it got better after every trip. With walking, that bulb where his toes had been flattened out until he was able to wear shoes again. He still walked with a bit of a limp, but Jim felt that in time he would overcome it and walk as he did before he was wounded. One morning the orderly dropped a note on his bed. It told him to report to Orthopedics to get a Metacarpal Bar for his foot. Jim asked me if I knew what it was. I told him that I didn't have the slightest idea. I had never heard of such a thing before. This set Jim worrying again. We had seen and heard of all kinds of metal surgical implants to correct bone problems. Jim thought it meant more surgery, but I told him no, that if it was surgery, the meat wagon would come for him. He was still worried when he left for Orthopedics, but in less than a half an hour he was laughing and pointing to the shoe on his half foot. He sat down on the bed and showed me the sole of his shoe. Right across the sole where the ball of his foot would have been was a leather bar about a half-inch wide and a quarter-inch thick. This was the Metacarpal Bar. With this and filler for the empty front of his shoe where his toes had been, all signs of a limp were gone.

Jim and I became good friends during that month or so we spent in that hospital in England. I finally got my long promised ride back to the States, leaving Jim still there in England. However, one day months later as I was leaving the Rehab Center of Walter Reed Army Medical Center in Washington, D.C., I looked over and was there Jim sitting on the big porch in a deck chair watching the coming and going. We immediately continued the friendship and Jim often came home with me to enjoy a home cooked dinner at my family table or sometimes just to sit around the living room and chat with Mom and Dad. After Jim went home to New Jersey we kept in touch by letter and Christmas card, but somewhere along the line I lost track of him. I do know he got married to a very nice looking young lady and that funny foot became only a reminder of a very close call he had while serving his country during World War II.

LIFE IN THE
QUONSET HUT WARD

Life in that Quonset ward in England went something like this. The morning usually started with a wet washrag being dropped on your face by the nurse or ward boy, then a little washing, breakfast and the medical rounds. After the doc had left Louie Prima and his Band of the ETO. It always started with his hit and theme song "Robin Hood." It was well liked by us and most knew it by heart. Sometimes during the day, if things were becoming boring, one would "Da, De, Da" the first few notes. Some would do the same to a few more notes and around the ward it went. Another song that was played a lot over the P.A. system was a Western song entitled "Don't Fence Me In." I can't remember who sang it on that record, but it sure made us think of home even though we were not cowboys. The "Don't fence me in" part also made us think of comrades not as fortunate as us who were in a German POW Camp.

The Red Cross was put down by a lot of veterans following the war. The biggest complaint, at least that I heard, was that they were charged for coffee by Red Cross vans up near the combat zone. Some claimed they never got anything from the Red Cross with out paying for it. I don't know about such things. General Patton kept us moving on the Moselle-Saar Valley drive that even our gasoline and ammunition had a hard time keeping up with us. There was no time or place for Red Cross or USO. I sure can say that the Red Cross was sure nice to have around in the hospital, particularly across the sea in England. The service I liked best was the book cart that came around daily with books from the military base's library. I think I must have read every book that they had. The Red Cross also brought craft items around. They furnished me with watercolor paints, brushes and paper. I filled in many an hour that would have otherwise been boring painting scenes of Noville from memory. A real fun thing I did was to make a felt duck and stuffed doll that looked like Pinocchio. I had never sewn before, except my uniform patches, but both the duck and doll turned out real nice. I gave the duck to our day nurse, Swanee, and many years later dug Pinocchio out of Mom's cedar chest and gave it to my daughter, Sharon. I also would not have had a razor or toothbrush if it had not been for the Red Cross ladies.

There were patients on the ward from all parts of the United States and although this was an orthopedic ward, wounds varied as much as hometowns. Most were combat wounded, but a few were there after having broken bones in accidents. Those with minor injuries stayed about a month and then were shipped back to their outfits or new duty. There was a good group of amputees who, like me, were waiting for a ride back to the States for another operation to remove scar tissue from their stump and then to be fitted with an artificial limb. The ward had a few with more than one wound that were in serious condition. These were usually flown out as soon as the doctor thought they could stand to travel. In February they brought in a tanker who was in critical condition from wounds all over his body. When a tank gets hit you have more then just shrapnel to contend with. Nuts, bolts, and all sorts of sharp pieces of metal shook free from the blast go round and round inside the tank. Most are killed by these sharp pieces of steel. This tanker was alive, but unconscious. His body was covered with nasty wounds and still filled with nuts and bolts, the ones that had not been in vital areas. He got a nice warm bed by one of the pot-bellied stoves and close care from the nurse and ward attendant.

This was winter in England and the weather had turned very cold and one night we had a bad snowstorm. Now in England, the rain and snow don't fall straight down, but blows in horizontally, pushed by the winds off the Atlantic. In the morning I woke up with snow all over my bed. It had been blowing in through a crack where the wallboard had slipped down. I used some string to lace the siding back up and covered the rest of the crack with adhesive tape. Those two pot-bellied stoves were having a hard time keeping that big drafty Quonset hut warm. The ward boy was kept busy going out into the storm to get coal. I helped by keeping the fires going and letting the ward boy know when the coal supply was getting low. That night, things got worse. The wind blew, the snow flew and it got colder and colder. Keeping those cast iron stoves hot enough to do any good consumed the coal at a faster and faster rate. One time the ward boy came back in with the scuttle still empty. He told me if there was any coal left out back, he couldn't find it as everything was drifted over with snow. He added that he was going to main supply for some and asked me to do my best to keep the fires going. He pointed to the very sick tanker and said, "Watch him, please."

The fire in the stove by the tanker got low and the other one was down too so I banked to make it last longer and went back to the one keeping our very sick patient warm. I looked at him and he didn't look very good. The nurse was over in the other hut and our phone line was down. We had wooden folding chairs all through the ward. They were ones just like my church used for special occasions. I started breaking them up and got some of the guys to help. The wood burned a lot faster than coal, but kept the place good and warm. The ward boy finally got back with coal. A truckload was dumped outside the front door. The tanker was operated on the next day. He had had a close call that night, but was going to make it. We got new chairs after the storm died down and no one ever said anything about me destroying government property. I had been afraid that they might make me pay for them by deducting the cost from my paycheck. That would have taken a long time for a PFC's pay was only some $60 a month.

There was a young red headed kid in the first bed in the row on the other side from me. I never knew his name as everybody just called him "Red." He had a light complexion and a set of freckles to go with his red hair. This with his freshly washed look made him appear younger than he actually was. To most he looked no older than sixteen. Most of us were young and none were old. I was still nineteen. This upset my mother when she came to visit me after I got back to the States. She kept commenting on how young everyone on the ward looked. I finally said to her, "Mom, you can't fight a war with old men." Red was bashful and quiet there in his corner, but right after lights-out he surprised everyone with an excellent imitation of President Roosevelt giving one of his "Fire-side" radio talks. He knew one of these talks by heart and recited it every night. He put special emphasis on the part where our President said, "...our boys will NEVER fight on foreign soil."

One night sometime after midnight Red woke up screaming in pain. The nurse and ward boy came running. She checked him and then went to his charts. A doctor was called and after a brief look at Red they rushed out of the ward on a "meat wagon." By now, everyone on the ward was awake with most wondering what had happened to this nice quiet guy who had seemed to be doing so well. In the morning they brought Red back to his bed on the gurney. He was higher than a kite and was signing "The Man on the Flying Trapeze" at the top of his lungs. He hadn't been drinking. It was the anesthetic. The

Army used a kind of sodium anesthetic that in some people produces the symptoms of being on a happy drunk. On me, it put me out in just a few seconds. I don't know how I might have acted because I don't remember anything and no one told me of my behavior. Red was having a ball! When Swanee came to help him into bed, he greeted her with a big smile and blurted out, "Hello Honey. How about a kiss?" It was so out of style for the soft spoken Red that we couldn't help laughing. He didn't notice us, just the nurse.

Finally he fell to sleep. When he woke up he didn't re-member any thing about his behavior and blushed beet-red from head to toe. Every time Swanee came anywhere close to his bed he hid under the covers until she left. We got him talking about what had happened and he finally got over his embarrassment. Red explained that when they took care of his wounds they left one bullet in his back to be removed at a later date when he had gotten some of his strength back. It was clean and in a safe place, but last night it started moving. It had hit his backbone and was forcing its way between two vertebrae heading for his spinal cord. They got it out in time and Red got better and left us for a hospital back home.

One day a couple of men all dressed in white pushed a cart on to the ward and up to my bed. The cart had buckets and a box on it and a lot of white stuff over everything. The white stuff was plaster and they told me that they had come to put a traveling traction cast on my stump. The traveling part sounded great as I had been waiting several months to be sent back to USA. This was a long time considering that when I was shipped from France I had been told that I would be headed home within two weeks. However, I did not like the idea of a traction cast as I had been out of traction for well over a month and my stump had completely healed over. They agreed that it was silly, but they had their orders and the Army had its

regulations that said an amputee had to be shipped in a traction cast. They went to work and when they had finished, I had
more plaster wrapped around me than a person with major
broken bones. I had no broken bones.

The cast not only covered my stump, but also came up
and around my waist. I couldn't even move my right hip joint
an inch. From the inside of the cast came a long thick wire. It
went out for about eighteen inches then crossed over and came
back to the outside of my cast. Like on my original skin traction
a cloth tube had been glued to my skin. Now if I had needed
traction there would have been an elastic cord tied around
the cloth tube and stretched down to the end of the wire. This
would keep pulling the skin down and over to cover the end
of my stump. Since my stump was healed over they skipped
the elastic cord, but I still had all of that plaster to lug around.
Before they left they put a curved sheet of metal over me that
covered my bottom half. It looked like a small Quonset hut, but
it was a heater to dry the plaster. I was in that oven most of
the day. The nurse came to turn me at intervals so the plaster
would harden on all sides. Even in this cool ward this oven had
me sweating and miserable. Just before dinner the nurse came
again to check me out. This time she said I was done. She was
right. I was done. All the plaster was hard as a brick and on
my right side from the waist down I was stiff. I couldn't move
anything at all.

Not being able to move my right hip and the extra weight
of the cast made getting out of bed difficult, but out of bed I
must get to answer nature's call. Walking to the bathroom on
crutches that first time was a bummer, but I made it. I also now
knew why a turtle had such a slow gait. Now that I was in the
bathroom and looking at the toilet, I wondered how in the Hell
I was ever going to fit on the pot. I backed into the stall to give
it a try and discovered that I wouldn't fit sitting down due to the

long wire thing unless the stall door was open. I got the door held open with a trashcan against it. I went at it again and by holding the side rails in the booth I was able to lower my ass on to the round seat. The rest of the job was very painful. Something about a bowel movement sends signals to every nerve in the body and when these signals hit the end of my stump, Oh Boy, Oh Boy!

I made it back to my bed OK, but it was a struggle. I could get used to the weight, I thought, but the stiff hip and right side would sure slow me down. I had hoped that maybe sooner or later the doctor would change his mind and let me have a pass so I could take a look at this historic British town of Oxford. I had asked before and had been turned down. The ward boy told me that the doc wouldn't let any patients using crutches leave the hospital grounds, as he was afraid they would fall and hurt themselves and this would look bad on his record. He didn't realize, or care, that this was probably the only chance that most of us would ever have to see anything of England. I had been trying to organize a "great escape" by cutting a hole in the chain-link fence and heading out across the golf course and into town. Of course this was all in our heads, but I wondered if the good doctor had gotten wind of it and had ordered this cast to stop any such plans. If so it worked. There was no way I could ever wear a uniform with this contraption on me and I sure didn't want to go sight seeing in my Army issue PJs.

That night long after lights out, I was still trying to find a comfortable position for sleeping. I had just concluded that there was no such position when I heard the door open and shut. I knew it was the day ward attendant. We had become friends and sometimes when he returned from a night out on the town he would bring me a Tom Collins in a paper cup. I was right. It was he. He headed for my bed and before I could warn him he sat down on the bed. He sat right on top of my new cast

(It had been his day off and he did not know about my latest GI attire). His weight cracked the plaster at my hip. He jumped up in surprise. I told him about the cast and he said, "Oh, Shit!" and left in a hurry. He wasn't supposed to be on the ward until 6 am and of course the Tom Collins was against regulations also. After he left I drank the Tom Collins, I had to get rid of the evidence. Ha, ha, It tasted good and helped me to get to sleep.

The next morning when I went to get out of bed I found that the crack in my cast made it a lot easier. I now had the use of my hip joint back and could move my plaster-covered stump around with a fair amount of ease. No one ever asked me how my brand new cast had gotten broken and I never told anyone. It was a secret between the ward boy and me. I looked down at the traction wire and wondered if I could stand on it and maybe even walk. It looked strong enough, but it was a few inches short of being long enough. Next to my bed was a folding wooden chair like the ones I had burned on that cold snowy night. I noticed that the rung between the two back legs was about five inches from the floor. I stood behind the chair and put the cast wire on it. It was a perfect fit. I found that both the cast and wire were strong enough to support my weight. The chair slid forward on the smooth ward floor and I followed. I pushed forward, the chair slid and I followed. I had discovered a wheelless scooter and around the ward I went, free of crutches. No one said any thing about my new mode of transportation. The patients cheered me on. The nurse didn't complain as it freed up a set of crutches and marks made buffed away during the daily cleaning.

One of the highlights of the week was the arrival of the "Stars and Stripes" newspaper. It was the Army newspaper for the ETO, European Theater of Operations. It was our main source for news about how the war was going in Europe. Although the news was of a general nature so as not to give any useful information to the enemy, most of us could figure out where our outfit was and what it had been doing to help end the war. It also gave us other news about the war and home front and usually was our only source for this information. The cartoons were always a favorite part of the Stars and Stripes. There was the now famous "Sad Sack," GI Joe, better known as "Private Breger," and my favorite, "Up Front" featuring those dirty, haggard infantrymen "Joe and Willie." That was me. That was what we looked like and they way we thought and looked at life and, yes, death. Whenever someone asks me what war was like, I tell him or her that to know the true answer to that question one has to be there and experience it day after day. However, I add that the books "Brave Men" by Ernie Pyle and "Up Front" by Bill Mauldin will give them a closer feeling of what the combat of war was like.

Whenever I could, I clipped an "Up Front" cartoon and mailed it home. Now many of these panels had humor only a combat GI could understand. My mother couldn't see anything funny about them and wondered why anyone would draw such dirty old characters. When I got home and explained to her that was a true picture of how it was with her son and all of the rest of the men on the front lines she also became fond of them. She found it hard to believe that her teenage son ever looked like "Joe and Willie," but on my 20th birthday she handed me a copy of "Up Front."

Word finally came that I was going back to a hospital in the USA for final surgery and to be fitted with an artificial leg. No, I wasn't going to be flown there, but would cross the Atlantic once again by boat. I was so glad to hear the news that I really didn't care how they sent me. The ship was OK by me. I had never been in an airplane before and feel more secure on the water than in the air. The import thing was that after many promises, my time had come. I was goin' home!

BACK TO THE STATES AT LAST

An ambulance took me from the Quonset hut hospital to the train station in Oxford. There I was put on a British hospital train. It looked like the one I had been on for my New Year's Eve ride to Oxford, and it probably was. This time the trip was the reverse of my first ride as I was now going back to the port of South Hampton. I didn't get much of a look at the ship, but it was a hell of a lot bigger than the fishing boat that had brought me across the English Channel. I was carried up a sturdy gangplank, across the deck and down a flight of stairs. On a ship all stairways are called ladders. The ones on the fishing craft were just that, but on this vessel they looked like stairs in any building that I had ever been in.

We arrived at a brightly lit compartment full of bunk beds in tiers of four. They ran around each wall and there was a group of them in the middle of the room. I was placed on a bunk against the far wall and about half way up the tier. I don't remember any of the bottom bunks being used. The room was bright and clean. The brightness came from the electric lamps, as there were no windows – I mean portholes – in the room. We were not allowed to get out of bed even to walk around the room to stretch our legs and it was back to the bedpan and duck. There was no way to tell if it was day or night. The nurse flicked the switch and made it day or night, but we never knew if it was for real. It took 14 days to reach New York City. It was a smooth but boring trip.

The only excitement we had during this time came from a Greek kid from Brooklyn. He was in one of the center bunks.

Shell fragments had hit him in the back and had left him para-
lyzed from the waist down. It is a terrible feeling to have the
lower half of your body dead and useless. It wasn't not being
able to walk that worried Pete the most. It was: Would he be
able to have sex? Could he get a hard-on? He talked about this
all the time, but we couldn't be of much help. One morning
when the lights went on Pete began to holler, "Look, look!" over
and over again. The sheet over his lower half was standing up
like a circus tent. He had an erection. He was so happy he was
crying with joy as he hollered, "Look, look, look!" The nurse
and attendant came rushing expecting to see some terrible ac-
cident. When they saw Pete's tent and him pointing at it, they
burst out laughing. We all laughed and cheered for Pete's tent. I
think Pete was the happiest man I have ever seen. It also meant
that feeling in the rest of his body was going to return.

With nothing much to do but lay down, there was a lot
of time for thinking. What I thought about most was how was
I going to tell Mom and Dad that I had lost my leg. They only
knew that I had been wounded in my leg. In my letters I was
not allowed to give any details of where I had been or how I
had been wounded. I just told her I was feeling fine, getting better all of the time and would be coming home soon. I worried
how she would take it and hoped she would feel as I felt: I was
damn lucky to be alive. She would worry about my feelings and
me, but when I talked to her she would be able to tell that I was
eager to get fixed up and to get on with living.

I also wondered what an artificial leg looked like and how
it worked. I had never seen one except for the peg leg on Long
John Silver in the movie "Treasure Island." I felt that I could
and would get around on one as well as anyone and would be
able to do the important things like getting from here to there. I
would miss football. I liked the game and was pretty good at it
in high school, but I did not think I was big enough to play on

any college team. What I would miss the most was running. I had always enjoyed running and had been on both my junior and senior high schools' track team. I was good at it. In fact at the high school level of competition in the Washington, D.C. area, I had been the first to do the 100-yard dash in less that 10 seconds. I did it in 9.9. It didn't go into the record book as I did it in a heat and not a final event. It would have been nice but not a necessary part of my college life still to come.

The ship pulled into the harbor at New York City. Two U.S. Army men came – no German POWs this time – and gave me a stretcher ride to the deck and down the gangplank where they put me into an ambulance. It was bright and sunny. Boy was it good to see the light of day and blue skies after two weeks inside that ship. Now it hit me! Not only was it a beautiful sunny day, but also that beautiful sky was hanging over the good ole U.S.A. I was home at last. What a great feeling. The ambulance took us to a tall hospital located just outside the city at Camp Shanks. Camp Shanks had been my P.O.E., Port of Embarkation, so I had come back to where I had started my tour of Europe. It was evening by the time I got to my bed in this "high-rise" hospital. A ward attendant came up to my bed and told me a steak dinner was on the way for my evening meal. Wow! I hadn't seen steak since I left home for the Army. Just a couple of months ago in Noville I was happy to have a box of K-Ration and now a steak dinner with all the trimmings.

A few minutes later a Red Cross lady came over to me carrying a telephone. She asked me if I would like to call home. I said yes, and she handed me the phone while she dialed the number I gave her. The phone rang only once. My mother answered. The call went through just as fast as if I had been right next door to her, and she must have been standing close by to answer so quickly. I said, "Hello Mom. I'm here in New York." She didn't seem too surprised, but I guess she had been waiting for my call ever since I had written her from the hospital in England. After hello and welcome home she asked how my leg was doing. I told her to brace herself, for I didn't have my leg anymore. I quickly added that when she heard where I had been and what had happened she would know that I was very lucky to be here at all. She simply asked if I had been at Bastogne, and I told her yes. She said from reading the newspaper, we thought you might have been there. We talked some more then she asked, "I guess you'll be coming to Walter Reed."

Walter Reed Army Hospital was only two blocks from my home on Geranium Street. I said, "Mom, that would be the logical hospital, but you should know the Army by now. I could just as well wind up in California." Now mother and dad had lived in Washington, D.C. most of their lives and had many friends in many places. Several times she had written me with opportunities to get out of the infantry. I had replied thanks, but no thanks. I like it where I am. I was proud of my blue braid. However now I said to her, "If you still have any strings you can pull to get me in Walter Reed now is the time to pull it." My time was up so I told them that I loved them, would soon be home to tell them the whole story and again that I was doing fine.

They came and cut the cast off of me and gave me a pair of crutches that were all my own. I went to the bathroom to clean up and get rid of some of the plaster dust that still clung to me. I even shaved with the plastic razor the Red Cross had given me in England. I looked in the mirror and saw that I had gained weight and had lost that tired gaunt look of a combat soldier. I had also gotten rid of the bloodstains that had turned my hands and arms black. I needed a haircut and would get one as soon as I could. One of the patients told me that a barber came to the patients on the ward. It would be nice to greet mom and dad looking as good as possible. I had been mad that my trip home had been postponed for such a long time, but it turned out to be a good thing as for several weeks over there I looked like the Hell I had been through.

The next morning after medical rounds I asked for permission to go to the canteen. I signed out and was pointed in the right direction by the ward attendant. As I walked on my crutches down a long hall, I looked out of a window and down below. Across the way I saw the barracks where I stayed with other 10th Armored Tigers while waiting to board the ship that would take us to join Patton's Third Army. It seemed like that had been years ago. I turned a corner and knew I was getting close to the canteen as I could hear music spilling from a jukebox out into the hall. The tune was new to me, but I recognized the voices of the Andrew Sisters.

As I swung through the door on my crutches I could hear the words the Andrew Sisters were signing. The song was "Rum and Coca-Cola." If the jukebox had not been turned way up, no one could have heard it. The place was packed full of soldiers just back from overseas. They were making a racket, a happy racket of voices glad to be back in the U.S.A. again. It was so smoky that it reminded me more of my local "gin mill" than an Army canteen. It also reminded me that I had not smoked a cigar for quite some time. I preferred cigars, but cigarettes were more suited for a short smoke. As much as I enjoyed a good cigar, no one, including me, likes the smell of a dead one lying in an ashtray. I decided to have a cigar and a coke. They didn't sell beer. Some how I got through the crowd and got my cigar and coke. I was looking for some place to sit down and enjoy them when a patient in front of me said, "Hi! Have a seat. Just get back?" I told him yes and sat down. The Andrew Sisters were singing so loud I could hardly hear him over the tones of "Rum and Coca-Cola." I finally gathered that he was talking about a shoebox he had in front of him. He opened it and took out a fifth of rum and poured a shot in my coke.

I joined the merry throng and toasted my return to the U.S.A. as the Andrew Sisters sang on and on. I think that was the only song that got played all day. At least that was the only song I heard while I was there. It was also the first music I heard on my return home. It's still a favorite of mine. I looked through the smoke and saw by the clock on the wall it was time for me to head back to my ward. As I passed some large doors on my right, I heard a faint sound of music. I stopped and pulled on the door handle, and it opened. I opened it enough so I could look in and saw an auditorium with lots of patients and other people watching a stage show. From my angle I could not see the stage or the performers, but the song they were singing really grabbed me. The song was, "You got to Accentuate the Positive, Eliminate the Negative and don't mess with Mr. In-between." I knew those words were meant for me and for the beginning of my new life on one leg. I took it to heart and made it my theme song. It was like the good Lord had sent me a message. I shut the door and continued back to my ward feeling much better and ready to face anything that might come along.

I didn't stay at the Camp Shanks Hospital very long – not more than two days. I left it with a large group of patients, and we were transported to a nearby train station. We were loaded on an Army hospital train. It had a large white stripe running the full length of the train, and at the center of each car there was a large red cross. We still had not heard where we were going, but when my car was full a man up at the front announced in a loud voice, " This car is going to Walter Reed Army Hospital in Washington, D.C." I yelled whoopee so loud that every head swung around to look at me. The man who had made this wonderful statement said, "It sounds like you are going close to home soldier!" I answered, "You bet I am!" Mother's "string" had really worked, as this was the only car in the entire train going to Walter Reed. Some patients near me asked how close, and when I said two blocks I don't think they believed me.

My train pulled into Union Station in Washington and my car was detached and shuttled around the rail yard until it was hooked to an engine going north on the B & O line. The one car train was headed west like it was going to Chicago, but that was also the way to get to Silver Spring, Md. a border line town to D.C. and not far from Walter Reed. When we reached Silver Spring the train backed down a siding that ran almost into Georgia Avenue, the town's main drag. There was a small crowd of people gathering to watch the arrival of the hospital train. I knew right where I was as I had often watched trains unload on this same siding. Not many trains used this siding anymore, and an Army hospital train was a special event. A group of Army ambulances were parked by the siding waiting for us. As I was being carried out of the train I looked at the group of people, and then to my amazement I heard a voice calling loudly from the edge of the crowd. It was a girl jumping up and down calling my name as she waved at me. I recognized her right away. It was Jean Bartemire. She lived just three houses down from me on the corner of 16th and Geranium Street.

What a welcome home. My fellow passengers who had been a little skeptical as to how close I was coming to home were now true believers. They wanted to know if she was my girlfriend. I said no, just a family friend and neighbor. The trip down Georgia Avenue, across the District Line and to Walter Reed didn't take anymore than five minutes. Our convoy went in the Georgia Avenue entrance and around to the ambulance entrance at the west end of the main building. I was placed on a gurney and rolled down the main corridor of the hospital to the Registration and Information Desk by the main entrance to the building. As I was pushed down that hall it dawned on me that although I had often been through and on the grounds outside of the hospital, this was the first time I had been in it. We reached the registration desk, and the lady in charge was handed my medical record. She looked at it then turned to me and said, "Hello. So you are PFC Donald J. Addor. We have been waiting for you for some time."

I asked her how come, and she said that they had received many telephone calls asking if I was there and I had had a few visitors already. In fact, in the last month a general, a captain and a lieutenant had called at the desk to see me. She added that the captain had come several times and said he would be back soon. The lady gave me the list of my visitors. I read it as they pushed me up to Ward 10-A. Two of the officers I recognized as high school buddies from my graduation class of 1943. They were Captain Wilbur Wagner, a friend and fellow photographer, and Lieutenant Don Herndon who had been a schoolmate for many years. I didn't have the faintest idea who the general was, but his name sounded slightly familiar. There were other names that I recognized from my life before the war. The reason for the visitors and phone calls was that the Washington newspapers had run an article about my being wounded way back in January shortly after mother and dad had received the official telegram. I hadn't realized so many would be interested in my welfare.

This is the main entrance to Walter Reed Army Hospital in Washington, D.C. Its beautiful gardens attracted many tourists, especially in the spring.

Below: The man entrance to the Forest Glen, Md., convalescent section of the Army Medical Center

After I had gotten situated on the ward, I asked for a telephone. They brought me one and plugged it into a jack by my bed. I called home and mom answered the phone. I told her that I had arrived at Walter Reed, and she informed me that she already knew it and would be over as soon as visiting hours began in the afternoon. Jeanie Bartemire had rushed down to Geranium Street to tell mother that she had seen me coming off the hospital train. The whole neighborhood knew I was at Walter Reed before I had entered the Georgia Avenue gate.

My new ward was an orthopedic ward and most patients were leg amputees. The ward was on a three-story wing that jutted out from the front of the hospital. My ward, 10-A, was one story up. There were windows down both sides of the ward and a long open porch that ran the whole length. From this elevation I could see the large water fountain in the circle in front of the main entrance and the beautiful gardens that surrounded the hospital. At the end of the ward was a large day room with lounge chairs, tables and reading material. It was truly a beautiful place both inside and out, quite an improvement over the Quonset hut in England. Walter Reed was well established, nothing temporary about it, and was considered one of the best in the world. My mother had visited patients here during World War I. Many who had been her high school classmates and now many years later she was coming back to visit a patient. This time it was her son.

On the right side of my bed was a good-sized Italian named Tony Cerasaro. Tony had been here a long time. He had lost one leg, and the doctors were trying desperately to save his remaining leg. This had meant a long series of bone and skin grafts that sometimes didn't take and had to be done over again. In spite of this long ordeal he was a happy smiling patient who seldom complained. Tony and I loved cigars, and we made a smoky duo in that area of beds. Tony always had a lot of visitors, both family and friends, despite the fact that he hailed from Pennsylvania. Tony was there when I arrived at Walter Reed, and he was still there when I left in December. I don't know what finally happened, but I hope that doctors were able to get his remaining leg working again.

As soon as the afternoon visiting hours started mother came. It's hard to write down how I felt. Words are not adequate. We embraced and said the usual things that one says at such times, but there is no way that I know to express in writing the inner feelings we both had. It seemed like I had been away for years, but it had only been a little over eight months since I had been home on leave prior to going overseas. We talked about what had happened at home and with me. I told her how my 20th Armored Infantry Battalion had stopped the Germans outside of Bastogne two days before the 101st paratroopers even got to Bastogne. Of course I told her how I had been wounded between Noville and Foy and how lucky I was to have gotten back to my outfit. Yes, she realized how lucky she was to have her son back and was comforted by seeing that I was in such good spirits.

She did tell me that I needed a haircut and that my pajamas were too big. I agreed that a haircut was in order and that I had an appointment to get one tomorrow when the barber visited the ward. I explained that this was the best the Army had in PJs. Sizes came in too big and way too big, so mine was considered a perfect fit. We both laughed, and visiting hours were over. Mom left feeling that things were going to be different but OK. She added that she and dad would be back in the evening. After dinner mom was back, and dad was with her. He sure looked great! Before we started talking he handed me a little box. I opened it, and there was a Combat Infantry Badge in it. I had forgotten that while in England I had written home telling them that I had qualified for the CIB, and I asked them if they could buy me one as I didn't know when the Army would issue mine. There it was.

Mom said she went down town to Sports Center, a store in downtown Washington D.C., that sold sporting goods and military uniforms. The salesman had asked to see the official orders for it. I had not received them yet so she didn't have any to show him. However, when she showed him the letter I had written her about it and the postmark from the hospital in England, an exception was made, and mom was able to purchase the award. She said everyone in the store sent their best wishes. I am proud of all of my decorations but value my Combat Infantry Badge the most.

The first week at Walter Reed was quite busy. I had so many visitors that everyone on the ward was beginning to wonder who I was. I assured them that I was PFC Donald J. Addor, but this was just my hometown. The hospital sat right in the center of the neighborhood where I grew up. I had cut through the grounds on my way home from school and had listened to the bugler play taps from my bedroom on summer nights when the window was open. My first non-family visitor was Wilbur Wagner. He was a captain and pilot in the Army Ferrying Command. He said that ever since he had read about my being wounded, he had been flying to the D.C. area to check on me. That's why so many visits. Not only were we high school buddies, but we were also into photography. Wilbur was more advanced in photography than I was. In fact he had been offered a job with Life Magazine when he graduated, but he turned it down saying photography was his hobby and went to war in the Air Corps instead. He first asked me how I was and then asked how my camera was.

I told him my camera was gone. The Germans had either captured it or it had been burnt up with my half-track. I also told him that there was not much time for picture taking where

I had been, and the few that I had taken had also been captured while waiting in my barracks bag until I could get them developed and censored. Wilbur came back the next day and gave me his Argoflex that he had used in high school. He wouldn't take any money for it and said he had another camera now. I was very flattered and pleased as many award winning photos had been taken on that camera. Wilbur told me his new camera took 520 film packs, and he was having a hard time finding them. (All photo supplies were in short order due to the war.) I told him I just happened to have about a half dozen of them at home as that's what my camera had used. My cousin had married an officer who was in charge of all the Army photo schools, and he had sent them to me.

I don't remember the order of my visitors for the rest of that first week back home, so I'll just tell you about them as they come to mind. One afternoon a lieutenant walked up to my bed, and we shared warm greetings. This was Don Herndon also from high school days. We had been in the high school cadets together, and in our senior year he was the colonel and I was his captain and regimental adjutant. Like me he had been in the ASTP, an Army college program, and when it was discontinued he went to the 106th Infantry Division. This was the "green" division that the Germans had pushed their heavy armor through to start their offensive. Don had been lucky for most of that division had been killed or captured. We had a good old talk about that big German attack and about school days too.

When he got up to leave he asked me if there was anything I wanted. I looked down at his infantry boots and said I would like a new pair of combat boots. I told Don how we in the 20th AIB had waited for the new boot that was designed for us, but when they came to our division they were issued to our tankers. This was a couple of months before we went overseas. My unit didn't get the Infantry Boot until just before we were shifted up to Bastogne. My long awaited boots were hardly broken in when the doctor had cut the right one off me to take care of my wounded leg. I knew officers had to buy their uniforms while the enlisted were issued what was being worn at that time and place.

The Quartermaster at the hospital didn't even stock combat boots. I would be issued a pair of low cut shoes, the sensible and practical shoe for an amputee. I told Don that I didn't know if I would ever be able to wear the boots and walk using a wooden leg, but I still wanted a pair. Don said, " No problem," and came back with a pair in just a couple of days. They were rough on the outside with the smooth leather on the inside like my Army shoes had been. The early ones like the tankers got had the smooth side of the leather on the outside like most shoes and took a real nice shine. Rough though they may be, I was happy to have a pair. They hung on the wall at home for a couple of years then one day during a snowstorm I tried them out. Even though it was a lot of weight swinging on the end of my wooden leg, I was able to walk in them. I used them for garden work and shoveling snow for many years.

The general who had come to see me before my arrival came back. I was correct. I did not know him, but he was in my outfit, the 10th Armored Division. He was Brigadier General Kenneth G. Aulthaus and until recently had been the Commander of Combat Command A. For fighting purposes the division had been divided into two teams, CCA and CCB. My 20th AIB and I were in Combat Command B, and the headman was Colonel William L. Roberts. I didn't know Col. Roberts, just that he was our leader and on occasions came and gave us a pep talk. The brigadier general had read my name in the newspaper and saw I was a 10th Armored Tiger. We talked until dinnertime about the war we had both left behind. Brig. Gen. Aulthaus' visit illustrates the great spirit of my division. Here was a general coming to see a PFC and when we got together we were both just two "Tigers" swapping experiences.

A Captain Roberts also visited me. I did not know him either, but like the general, he had read of my being wounded and that I had been with the 10th AD. His brother was Col. Roberts, the commander of my Combat Command. He had come from his desk in the Pentagon to see how I was and hear how his brother was doing. I kind of chuckled and said: "Captain, your brother is too far up the chain of command for a PFC to associate with, but just before we moved up to Bastogne he came and gave my outfit a nice talk and congratulated us on the fine job we were doing. He looked fine and sounded even better." I added that all the men under him liked him and thought he was a great leader. That made the captain feel good and made me feel good too for what I had told him about his brother was the truth and not B.S.

I Begin my Rehab at
Walter Reed AMC

I only stayed about a week on the ward at the main section of Walter Reed Army Medical Center in northwest Washington, D.C. I was then transferred to the WRAMC Rehabilitation Center at Forest Glen, Md. This was just a short distance from the D.C. line and was located in what had been a private girls school of some class before it was sold to the Army after we got into the war. The school's main building was a rambling affair that looked like a Swiss or Austrian mountain lodge. Instead of clinging to the side of the Alps, it was situated in the center of large woods made up of mostly big oak trees.

Attached to the front of this rustic building was a large porch that could easily be classified as a veranda. It was a wonderful place for the patients to sit and relax watching the many squirrels and birds or the visitors coming and going. Scattered through the trees all around the building were houses designed to represent homes from around the world, including a Japanese pagoda and a Spanish rancher. In the school days these had been sorority houses, but now most of them served as quarters for officers with families. "The Glen," as it was referred to, was truly a unique and interesting place and well suited for a rehab center.

It brought back a lot of memories to me. I had often come out here when it was full of girls to participate in dances and to give the ladies the eye. It had been owned by one of my high school friend's father and uncle. John had asked me to join him on a visit at the school because being all girls they needed more dance partners. It was great fun at first, but soon it got to be rather boring. Things were too formal, and the school had their students on a very short leash. This meant that at the end of the dance or party a formal goodbye was said, and we were hurried out. Now what our crowd liked to do after a dance or party was to pile into our jalopies and head to the Hot Shopee down on Georgia Avenue by the District Line. No chance of that with these girls, so we soon dodged the request for our presence whenever we could.

The place was different now with Army uniforms and olive drab colors where the young ladies and their teachers used to be. Under the new military surface the old charm that had been built into the school showed through. "The Glen" was connected to the main hospital by Army shuttle busses that ran on regular schedules all day long and into the evening. Getting into the city was easy as once at the main section you could take a D.C. bus or streetcar, or a taxi if you had the money. Actually the cab didn't cost too much if a group went together and split the fare. However, since I lived only a couple of blocks from the hospital my mom usually came out to get me in the family car. Mom did the getting as dad was still at work when I got off. Of course mom filled the car up with all those who could squeeze in, and it became a regular thing every evening. Some of the patients even spent some of their off-time at my house enjoying just sitting around a real home and listening to favorite radio shows on the big, floor-standing RCA.

This was fun. I enjoyed going home for dinner and out to one of the local taverns later in the evenings for a beer or two and to be with the gathering of friends coming home from the war. However, I was out here at "The Glen" waiting for a bed and surgery down at the main section. I needed some minor surgery on my stump to remove scar tissue and shape it out for fitting of prosthesis. This couldn't be done during the amputation in Paris or during my stay in the hospital at Oxford, England due to wound drainage and the possible presence of gangrene gas. It was considered a simple and routine operation. I wasn't worried about it, just eager to get it done so I could get fitted with an artificial leg.

I had been watching other amputees on the ward learning to walk again and was anxious to give it a try. I knew I could never run on the track team again, but to be able to walk without crutches and to look whole again was my goal. It would be great to have my hands free again. In the meantime I was enjoying myself being home.

There was a guy in a bed not far from mine who had been walking on a peg leg for some time. This was no ordinary peg leg, but it looked just like one. The difference was that at the location of the knee, there was a platform that kind of swiveled on an axis. John's leg was off below the knee, but in the time it had taken to get him to a hospital and to heal his stump; his knee joint had frozen from lack of use. John put his partially bent knee on this platform, strapped on the leg, and as he walked the pressure slowly bent his knee back until it was working all the way again. It sounded painful to me, but John said it didn't hurt at all. The other day he had come back from orthopedics with the peg under his arm strutting his stuff on a new full-fledged Army issue leg. He threw the old leg under the bed, and there it stayed.

I had been eyeballing it for a while wondering if I could make it work for me. I had no knee, but with a little padding here and there I thought it might work. Finally I asked him if I could try it. He said sure. He didn't need it anymore and tossed it over to me. With a little diddling I finally had it strapped on me and was standing on it. It felt fine so I pulled on my hospital uniform pants, rolled up the right pant leg and took my first step without crutches since I was shot down on the muddy

Belgium cow pasture. Hey, this was great! After a few test runs around the room I headed out the door and down the hall to where there was a full-length mirror. There were several long mirrors around the ward so amputees could see how we looked and how we were doing as we practiced on our artificial legs. There was also one near the door to the outside so we could check how our uniforms looked before going out on pass.

At the mirror I couldn't say it looked so hot, but there I was standing up on two legs and it felt great. I did some more walking up and down the corridor and was feeling just like Long John Silver. My stump had been healed over for a month or more before I left England and there was no pain or discomfort at all. I was having a ball when the head nurse came steaming down the hall yelling at me. She asked me what I was doing. "Walking," I answered. This did not impress her. She told me in no uncertain terms to get my ass back to my room before I hurt myself. Well, she was a captain and I was a PFC and an order is an order so back I went. She grabbed the leg and went off with it, but not before telling me all the bad things that could have happened to me. I never saw that leg again, but the feeling of walking on it stayed with me forever; I became even more anxious for my time to come.

My turn for the operating room and my stump revision finally came. I packed up my things, said goodbye and climbed on the shuttle bus for the main section. On arrival I was told to report to Ward 10-A. This was the same leg amputee ward I had been on when I first arrived. I set up house keeping by putting my stuff in the little bedside table and flopped down on the bed. There wasn't much to do but wait for the next morning when my operation was scheduled. I was talking to the guy in the next bed. He had been wounded in the Pacific Theater and was having a hard time of it. He needed a lot of skin grafts, and they can take a long time to work and be very painful. Again I felt very lucky.

I was surprised and pleased to see a ward worker roll in a cart full of bottles of ice-cold beer. This happened every afternoon at about teatime. Each patient was allowed two bottles, but it was an unspoken rule that you took your two bottles even if you didn't drink the stuff. There were a few who didn't. These extra bottles were passed on to the patients that had been confined to their beds for a long time. Some, like big Tony, had been on the ward for over a year. It was a hot day, and there was no air conditioning in the enlisted wards. I drank mine and enjoyed it thoroughly. Later on I would pass at least one of my bottles over to Tony and save my drinking for in town.

Early the next morning I was awakened by my nurse dropping a cold, wet washrag on my face. It did not startle me, as this seems to be the standard proceeding for greeting a patient in the morning. It had been the same at the hospital in Oxford, England. Of course this was done with only those patients that were not seriously ill. "Good morning," she said in a cheery voice and told me to wash up from the bowl she had set on the white porcelain stand by the bed. I was washing my face when she came back and stuck a needle in my upper arm. I didn't think anything of it as I'd been getting shots and pills routinely ever since that medic had helped me off the battlefield. I had hardly felt it. She was a good nurse and knew how to give a shot.

Two guys dressed all in white came in and gave me a shave. Not my face but the area on my stump that was going to be operated on. There wasn't much there, but they said the area must be very clean and germ free for the operation. The nurse came over and asked me if I was sleepy. This was the second time she had asked me that question. I thought to myself, that's a stupid question. I had been asleep all night. In fact it was the longest that I had been in bed for quite some time. Then in dawned on me! She came over again to ask me, but before she could say anything I asker her, "Was that a shot of morphine you gave me?" She said yes it was, and I should be feeling sleepy. I told her that if they were waiting for morphine to make me sleepy, I'd never get to the operating room. I explained that it had quit working on me some time ago. I wasn't sure why, but maybe it was because I had been given so many shots to ward off the pain from the gangrene. It had been many months since I had needed anything for pain, but morphine still didn't work on me.

She left without saying anything and in just minutes two guys in white came in pushing a gurney. This was my ride to the operating room. I slid my butt over onto the "meat wagon," and we went down the long halls to the elevator. At Walter Reed, like in most hospitals, the operating rooms were always on the top floor. I guess this went back to the days when the main source of light was still the sun shinning through a skylight. Only one elevator went up to the top. It was long and skinny with just enough room for a gurney and attendants. There was a door at both ends. One of the pushers pointed to the door opposite the one I had entered and said, "That's the door you don't want. It goes down to the basement and the morgue." I don't know if he was trying to scare me or not, but if he was it didn't work. I had been in a morgue before, a temporary one. I knew this was a simple operation.

When we reached the top floor they rolled me out and into a room next to the operating room. Here a nurse walked over to me holding the biggest needle I had ever seen. It looked to me like it should have been for a horse, a very big horse, but it was for me. I was told to roll over on my side, and she shoved it into my backbone.

In spite of that needle's size, I hardly felt it going in or out. I had never had a spinal anesthetic before, and I hope I never have to have one again. I was lying there waiting for the numbness, lack of feeling, to take hold. It started in my toes and worked its way up. It was kind of scary feeling sensation slowly leave the lower half of my body. I wondered, what if feeling never came back. But I forced myself to think of other things. If that shot of morphine had only worked I would have been in dreamland dreaming sweet things. It did help me to have a better understanding and feeling for those guys that had been hit in the back and would probably be like this for all their lives. I also remembered that mortar shell fragment that had knocked me down in battle. Just an inch further to the right, and I'd have been like this or dead.

When my numbness had reached my waist I was ready, and they wheeled me into the operating room. In the hall my doctor and surgeon, Major De Santis, came over and greeted me. I liked the doctor very much. He had been a Battalion Surgeon in combat in the ETO. Not in my area, but close enough that we could talk about the battle in certain towns. This was also one of the reasons that I had so much confidence in him as an orthopedic surgeon. A doc serving at the front gets more experience with broken bones and smashed bodies in a day than a civilian doctor would usually get in a year or more.

The next time I saw the doctor, he had a mask on his face and was dressed in a light green operating room gown. I was staring up at a circle of bright lights. One of the masked figures hovering around the edge of this circle of lights stepped forward and started to erect a screen across my chest to block my vision of what was going to happen down there. I asked the doc if I could watch. His eyes gave me a surprised look. I explained to him that when I got out of the Army, I planned to go to college and take up medicine. He looked over toward a figure standing just outside the circle of light. The figure nodded its head and away went the screen.

From my viewpoint, flat on my back, I couldn't see very much of what was going on. However, Maj. De Santis explained each step he took. At one point he pulled out some long stringy things that looked like small, bloody ropes. He explained that these were the main nerves, and he was pulling them out so when they were cut and returned they would be far up in the end of my stump. This would reduce the chance of problems if they should grow a little as nerves usually do. It was strange. With no feeling due to the spinal and the arrangement of lights, I had no conception that this was happening to me. It was like I was watching someone else under the knife. It was also very interesting.

Everything went well, and I was soon on the "meat wagon" heading out toward the elevator. One of the green-clad figures that had been standing in the back followed me out into the corridor. He walked up and asked, "How are you doing?" The voice sounded familiar, and as he pulled his facemask down I saw to my surprise that it was my Uncle Lee, Leland Standford McCarthy. I was going to ask him how he got here, but he had left and joined the other person who was standing watching the operation. I remembered that Uncle Lee had told me when I first got to Walter Reed that he played poker with the Major General Shelley U. Marietta at Columbia Country Club every Wednesday.

Back in the elevator Maj. De Santis joined me for the ride down. He asked me what the Hell was going on. I asked him what he meant by that, and he explained that it was the first time he had ever seen the Commander of the hospital come to watch such a minor operation. I could see that he was worried so I eased his mind. I told him that the man with the major general was my uncle who wanted to see what was happening to his nephew. I went on to tell him how they played poker together in a poker club – a very exclusive club with a lot of VIP's in it including several generals and doctors from the Washington area. He said I should have let him know that they were going to be there. I told him it was a surprise to me too. I never saw the major general again.

Back on ward 10-A, I was put in a side room for those who have just been operated on. This was not an intensive care unit. It was for non-serious operations where the patients needed care and watching while their wounds healed. Here I joined two other guys who had been operated on this morning for similar reasons. I was placed on a bed in the middle with Jimmy Podany on my left and Irvin Aggatucci (I'm not sure of these name spellings as it's been a long time since I've seen them) on my right. Jimmy was an above the knee amputee – about mid-thigh with a fair amount of stitching done on his revision. Irv was also an AK amp a little higher up the leg than Jimmy. He had also had some internal surgery to repair damage to his innards. He had many stitches both inside and out.

To me it was interesting how many different ways a leg could be lost in a war. I was knocked down by a mortar shell then hit with a machine gun. One bullet went through the artery in the calf of my leg, and gangrene did the rest. Jim told me that if he had not been a chowhound he would have been dead, blown to bits. He was on a LST in the Pacific being transported to another island. It was lunchtime, and he was the first one finished. As he went out the door, a bomb made a direct hit in the galley and killed everyone still eating. He was blown out of the door, and his foot had been torn off. He floated in a life raft in the sea for a few days and got "saltwater gangrene" that resulted in the loss of his leg up high. Irv did not talk about his wound, so I don't know what got him.

We had been told to lie still so we would not break any stitches. It hurt Irv to move, so it was fairly easy for him to stay put. Jimmy was scared of breaking them and lay there stiff as a board complaining and asking the ward-help for this and that. He complained so much that one day his girlfriends brought him a baby rattle. Now that sounds like he was a stinker, but he was a very likable person and could even laugh at himself. Me, I was restless as could be. Being still was almost impossible, but I tried for the first couple of days.

Then I wiggled my stump around and even felt it through the bandages, and it felt fine. I knew how fast I healed, so I bummed a wheelchair, climbed out of bed and rolled myself back to the Day Room where I could shoot the breeze or read magazines. I got away with it the first time, but the next time I grabbed a wheelchair to go to the bathroom – I always hated bedpans and ducks – the nurse caught me. She escorted me back to my bed with some very strong reprimands. She also told me that she had heard I had been to the Day Room. This was a no-no. I tried to explain how quickly I healed and how good I felt, but she countered with a book of regulations and an order to stay in bed. Now since she was a captain and I was a PFC, I would have to obey my orders. However, to make sure I obeyed them, she made me hand over the lower half of my hospital PJ's. So I just waited, reading books and talking to visitors until the 10 days were up and the stitches removed.

When the time was up and the doctor came to remove the stitches, it turned out that Jimmy, who had tried so hard, was the only one with a broken stitch. However it was nothing serious, so we all had a good laugh. I'd like to add here that Jimmy's super-sensitivity that made him complain so much turned out to be a great asset in his chosen profession. After his discharge from the Army, he went to The Bolivar School of Watch Making under a special program the company had set up for veterans. Jim visited my mother and dad while still attending this school and told them the following story.

It seems he was home for the weekend visiting his parents. When he went up to his bedroom for a night's sleep, he was kept awake by the clock downstairs. He said it was going "tick" when it should have been going "tock." He got up in the middle of the night, went downstairs and took it apart on the dining room table. He got it to tick and tock in the right order and went back to bed, having a great night's sleep.

I didn't stay long on ward 10-A. It was back out to Forest Glen section again. Here I went to physical therapy.

During Rehab I Became
a Public Speaker

One day after my whirlpool treatment on my way back to my ward, I passed the auditorium. Down front by the stage a man was talking to a group of seated patients. Not having anything to do, I decided to see what was going on. The man was talking about a thing he called, The Paper-Trooper program. This was a paper salvage program for students in the Washington, D.C., schools. The program gave the young people a chance to participate in the war effort and help collect the much needed paper salvage. He showed us ribbons and certificates that the children would be awarded for their efforts. There was also an exhibit of how the armed forces used the salvaged paper. I recognized the box that held our C-Rations and the cardboard boxes that held K-Rations and some cardboard tubes that held artillery and mortar shells.

He was asking for volunteers to visit the schools and tell the children about the program with a bit of our war experience tossed in. He wasn't getting much of a response from the group of patients. I was about to leave when suddenly it sounded interesting to me. I put my hand up and told him that I would do it on one condition. When he saw my hand he was all smiles, but when he heard the words "on one condition," the smile changed to a frown. He grumbled, "What condition?" When I told him that I would only do it if I could speak at the schools I had gone to, he was all smiles again, and I had a new job.

That evening when I went home from the hospital for dinner, I told mom and dad about the program and that I was going back to the schools I had attended to talk about saving wastepaper. She was amazed that I would even consider such a thing. Before I went into the Army, the last place I would have wanted to be was on stage in front of a lot of people of any age. Thinking it over I was surprised too. I had been a guy who wanted to sit at the back of the class or anywhere but up in front. However, now I was eager to do so without apprehension. I guess fighting a war and almost dying really does change a person. I know I viewed everything in a differing light.

My first speech was at Whittier Grade School, and there were a few teachers still there that had taught me in my first years of school. After a warm welcome, I entered the stage and in front of me was a mass of eager young faces. I was beginning to have second thoughts, but it was too late now. After a brief introduction by the principal, it was my turn. I started with what outfit I had been with and told them about fighting Tiger tanks and getting wounded. Once I got started the words came easy, and I showed them round cardboard tubes that were used to ship artillery and mortar shells and other kinds of boxes for military things.

When I was through with my talk, I asked them to ask me about anything that they were uncertain about. One little girl asked me what a half-track was. Instead of answering it myself, I asked if anyone in the audience knew. At least half a dozen hands shot up. I picked one, and his description was great. He got a big hand from his peers. Another kid asked why we couldn't pick up and recycle the paper off the battlefield. I explained we were busy chasing the Germans back to Berlin and didn't have time. Besides if we stopped shooting to pick up stuff, we could get shot. I added that a lot was burned to keep us warm on cold nights.

I can say that my first public speaking experience was a success, a great success, with the teachers, students, the Paper-Trooper Program and myself. Once I got started relating my part in the Battle of Bastogne and Noville and how I was wounded, the rest came easy. The next day my photograph was in the Washington Star showing a group of kids and me with a cardboard container for an artillery shell. This was considered very good publicity for the salvage paper drive and helped to spread word beyond the schools where I had talked. The next talk was at Paul Jr. High School, and it went even better. Here again there were some teachers there that had taught me years before. To me it seemed longer ago than it really was.

The last speaking engagement was the best, for it was only two years since I had walked across the stage at Coolidge High School to get my diploma. Only two years, but so much had happened. However, as the principal and a group of teachers greeted me it seemed like yesterday. There were even some students that remembered me, for I was a senior when they were in their first year. It was truly a good feeling to be back in school again. What a change from the battlefields of Europe.

I had done all of this on crutches while awaiting an operation on my stump that would prepare me for an artificial leg. In the hospital such things were called prosthesis. I didn't mind walking on crutches. My arms were strong, and I could swing along at a pretty good gate. Some of the patients who had lost a leg or arm felt self-conscious about the missing limb and didn't go out very much. Not me! I was glad to be alive after such a close call with death. I felt lucky that I had come through the war with only a leg gone. I was determined that I was going to enjoy the rest of my life the best I could. If a few people stared and acted rude, so be it, for I met far more who were nice and caring.

My next job was selling Victory Bonds and Stamps. It was only a few days after I had received my artificial leg when I was asked to go to Elizabeth City, N.C., to speak to schools and some factory workers and explain that although the fighting was over, there was still a lot that needed to be done. I was not in Elizabeth City very long, just long enough to talk to the city's schools and to the workers of a factory. At the factory I spoke from the loading dock. At every place I got a wonderful reception, and I was told that I helped to sell a lot of Victory Bonds. The most important thing to me was that this was where I really learned to walk on my wooden leg. I was out by myself and had to walk until I could find a cab.

I spoke at many other places not only for Victory Bonds, but also for blood drives and sometimes just for entertainment at a luncheon. These engagements came through the hospital's Public Information Office. I got called a lot, as I was willing to go and was physically able. I enjoyed getting out and meeting people. It was more fun than hanging around the hospital after my PT classes. Early one morning a man from PIO woke me up. I usually wake up easy, but I had been out late drinking beer with my friend and fellow patient Victor Mapes. He said he was sorry, but it was an emergency. He had just gotten a request for an Army speaker at a luncheon at the Mayflower Hotel in downtown Washington, D.C., and said there wasn't much time. I didn't even want to get out of bed, but he kept insisting so I finally said I'd go if my friend Sergeant Victor Mapes could go too.

Mapes had been drinking with me, and I hoped that he would say no and we could go back to sleep. It didn't work out that way, and we were soon heading for the Mayflower (This is a very high class place for a sergeant and a private first class to be going.) No one had told us anything about what was going on except that we were to say a few words. I figured I would just tell them about the fighting at Noville and how I got wounded. When Vic told his amazing story of fighting the Japanese in the Philippines and his remarkable escape and survival, they would be satisfied and we could go home.

The Army car let us off in front of the grand hotel. The doorman opened the door for us, and we strolled into the plush lobby. We were directed to the ballroom and what a crowd met our eyes. Right away we knew this was something special, and we felt like fish out of water. A waiter was passing by with a tray of martinis and both Vic and I grabbed one. It went down smooth and easy. It helped. Over in one corner of the room we saw a couple of GI's talking together. One was a Navy ensign and the other was a lieutenant from the Marines. The young Navy officer was busy reading through the papers he held in his hand. The Marine held some in his hand and glanced at them occasionally. They saw us and came over our way. That's when we found out what all of this was about. This was a meeting between the Senate Committee on Compulsory Military Training – in other words the draft – and members of the press. Both the Marine and the Navy officer were proud that they had won an essay contest at their base for the privilege of being here to voice their views on whether the draft should be continued after the war. We didn't tell them or anybody else that we had been more or less dumped out of bed and told to get down here to say a few words. We put up a front like we had been picked special, and in a way we had as no one else was available. More martinis. Then someone announced that lunch was ready and Sgt. Victor Mapes and PFC Don Addor were ushered in and seated at the head table with the other two representatives of our military.

Both my partner and I had done a good bit of speaking, but never before such an audience and never on such a profound topic. We had usually just related our personal war experience and then answered a few questions mostly about combat. This was a whole different ballgame. There were senators seated down one side of the long table and members of the press representing newspapers and radio from all parts of the U.S. of A seated down the other. I was glad that the other two went first. While they were reciting their essays, we had a little time to think and maybe glean an idea or two from their oration. They were done and then Vic went. He was regular Army and had enlisted a couple of years before Pearl Harbor was attacked. He did a great job and presented some interesting points of view. His war experience had them all sitting bug-eyed with open jaws.

I was sweating it out still wondering what I was going to say when I realized that this subject fit me like a glove. It was about the young high school student who would be asked to interrupt his education or other plans for his future life. I was that with a few exceptions. I had enlisted when I was 17 and not drafted. I had had one semester of college as a pre-med student before I went on active duty. So my thoughts were more to the point. I didn't remember what I said at that time, but the quotes in the newspaper the next day sounded great. The gist of what I said was that although my education had been interrupted, I felt that with the maturity and discipline I had acquired during my service in the Army I would be a much better student with a real desire to learn and succeed.

That was my most upbeat or important speaking assignment. One of the most enjoyable experiences happened down in Richmond, Va. I was sent down there to demonstrate the need for money after the war was over thus the reason for buying Victory Bonds. I was quartered in a room in a private residence within the city and a short taxi ride to the Armed Forces Recruiting Office that was to be my working headquarters. When I reported to duty at the Army section, they were surprised. Walter Reed had sent me two weeks too early. Instead of sending me back, they decided I should just wait there until the starting date of my talks to the Richmond area schools.

I had been there a few days just hanging around and drawing cartoons, when there was a lot of activity across the hall in the Coast Guard office. A little bit later the CO from there came over and introduced a great, big guy who was wearing a Coast Guard officer's uniform. It was Jack Dempsey, one of the world's most famous heavyweight boxing champions. When I was growing up his name was as well know as Babe Ruth's. He was an officer in the Coast Guard Reserve to see what he could do to help his country during the war. After the introductions he hung around and we talked. He was interested in what I was doing and what I had done. He looked at his watch and said, " I have to go to participate in the arrival of an LST down at the waterfront." He added that it was the first time back from the war for both crew and ship and a "royal greeting" had been planned. He started toward the door then turned to me and asked if I wanted to come. I looked at the Sarge and captain and they said, "Why sure." So off I went with the great Jack Dempsey. Boy, was I flattered and excited.

We headed down to Richmond's waterfront in a couple of staff cars. I was with Jack Dempsey. I knew Richmond was on the James River, but I did not realize that ocean going ships could make it that far inland. But, there the LST was as big as life pulling in and tying up. Now between where we were and the part of the dock we wanted to be on was something very deep with a narrow catwalk across it. I think it was a lock but am not sure. I was not too experienced in walking on my artificial leg on regular ground, and the narrow walkway with nothing in the way of railings got to me on my first step. I hesitated or rather froze, then Mr. Dempsey's deep voice said, "Don't worry, I got you!" At the same time, his hand griped my shoulder and what a hand it was, one of the biggest I'd ever seen.

Confidence surged through me and across the lock we went. I had absolutely no fear of falling with that big hand and strong arm holding me.

I enjoyed the ceremony very much. I have always enjoyed military band music, and there was lot of that. On the way back Cdr. Dempsey asked me if I would like to join him that night at a Victory Bond movie premier. I had done one before in Baltimore. People buy a bond to get in to see the first showing of a Hollywood movie, and before it began an auction was held of items donated by local merchants. I told my war experience and explained some of my rehab and its costs including a demonstration of my wooden leg. I usually had been given some other prosthetic devices and medical items with a list of how much they cost and an approximate number of patients still needing help in hospitals throughout our country. That night everything went great with the big man front and center and me doing my bit. I didn't have any props, but I remembered enough to get the point across. Then the auction began, and we sold a lot of stuff as well as Victory Bonds.

During our question and answer session Jack Dempsey was asked if he thought he could beat Joe Louis, the current heavyweight champion. His reply brought a lot of oohs and ahs from the audience. His statement went something like this: "Why of course I could. I could lick him with one hand tied behind my back." Now Joe Louis was a great champ, a really big guy with a strong knockout punch. When the crowd had settled down from his remark, Dempsey smiled and said Joe Louis was a great champ. He added that he would not get in the ring with anyone and would not be a boxer if he didn't think he could beat him. He added that it was this mental attitude along with his physical abilities that brought him the victories that lead to the world championship. It was quite an experience for me. I don't remember what the movie was or if I saw it, but I'll never forget my experience with that world champion, not only in boxing but also in every other way.

I did many more speaking engagements for Walter Reed Army Hospital and the Army. These included helping many blood drives to reach their goals. In late July or August I was ready for discharge from the Army. I had received all of the medical treatment that I needed and was walking very well on my artificial leg. I didn't really need a cane for walking, but if headed downtown I would carry one to let people know I had a walking problem. This kept me from being run over by the fast moving crowds on city sidewalks. There was also a problem when crossing the streets. Some lights were not quite long enough for me to make it all the way across, and there was usually a driver who thought I could run the last couple of steps to safety. I'd point the cane at such a car, and the driver would get the idea and slow down for me to make a safe exit.

I was ready to go those three blocks home and to civilian life when a representative from the hospital's Public Information Office asked me if I would stay with the hospital and help wind up the Victory Bond Drive and help with some more blood programs. I was eager to get started on my new life and told the person I would have to think it over. I thought about it and came to the conclusion, "Hell, why not." I was home most every night and had no plans except to return to college in February. I liked what I had been doing and the feeling of still being able to help my country. I told them that I would stay a while longer but wanted to be out by Christmas. It was well worth it, and I was discharged on December 8, 1945 and had a great Christmas at home with my family.

A SHOW OF SHOWS

I didn't see many USO shows while I was in the service. Only part of one when I was sent back behind the frontline to get a bath and a small show in the Red Cross Hall at Walter Reed Army Medical Center. Until I was wounded I was on the frontline where there was no time for entertainment. Unlike Hollywood versions, entertainers were not sent as close to the enemy as my outfit was. They would be in danger and so would we if we tried to look at anything but the Germans in front of us. Our only entertainment was mail call, smoking and booze. Booze we made by starting up local stills as we ran the Germans out of town.

I don't know what happened while I was in the hospital near Oxford, England for those several months. We had entertainment on the ward by mostly local talent and it was most appreciated. When I got to Walter Reed, I was too close to home to pay much attention to what went on at the hospital. However, one morning on my ward out at Forest glen the guy in the bed across from me asked if I was going to the show in the Hall that afternoon. I said, "No, why?" He answered by saying that Gene Krupa was going to be playing his drums there. Right away I cancelled all other plans made or unmade. Gene Krupa was my favorite drummer. I liked him better than Buddy Rich or Cozy Cole. He kept that steady beat going no matter how fast his sticks were flying.

That afternoon I headed upstairs to the auditorium. I was still wondering at my luck since a show with such a star was usually done down at that main section, either in the Red Cross

Hall or out in the formal garden. It was a very hot day and this old building had no air conditioning. However, the high ceiling in the auditorium gave some relief. This room dated back to the girl school's hey-day and was fashioned after a famous opera house in Italy. When we were all seated the curtains parted and a band began to play. There was Gene Krupa up high in the center on the drums. It was a good show, but I don't remember much about it, as I was intently watching and listening to the drummer. Gene Krupa really did his stuff. I was elated! The stage was cleared all but Krupa's drums, and we were all about to leave.

Gene Krupa hollered out, "Hey! Would you like to hear some more?" Everybody turned around and grabbed a seat. He explained that he had no place special to go until a gig that night in downtown Washington, D.C. He said, "I'll need two volunteers to hold my drums from walking off the stage." Needless to say he got his volunteers. They sat on the stage floor, one on each side of the base drum and with their legs and feet held that drum relatively still. Krupa sat down and picked up the sticks. He started slowly and quietly and both speed and sound gradually increased. Boy, did he go to town!

It wasn't long before he was ringing wet with sweat, but on and on he played. He played on those drums for at least an hour – only him, the world's greatest drummer and his drums. While he played his mouth kept going like he was chewing something. I had noticed this before when I had seen him in concert in Washington's Capitol Theater. Some even accused him of chewing dope. They said, "No one could play like that without taking something." When he finally stopped, one of the patients asked him about it. He laughed and said that he was counting. He always counted while drumming. It helped him keep the rhythm going.

This show made up for all of those I had missed, big or little. It was an experience that has lasted a lifetime, for even today almost 60 years later I can still turn back my mind and hear him playing.

LEARNING TO WALK AGAIN

After the stitches came out of my stump, I went back out to "The Glen." Each day I rode the shuttle bus into the main section for physical therapy that consisted mostly of giving my stump whirlpool treatments and exercising it, sometimes with weights. This felt great. It was good to get some muscle tone back in my thigh, and it also helped my skin to toughen. I had always had a pretty tough hide that heeled quickly and this quality came in very good at this time. Finally I was sent to prosthetics to get fitted for a leg. Boy, was I excited! I wondered how it would go as my stump was different than most. I had my entire femur bone as my leg had been disarticulated at the knee. This made my stump long and thin but gave me a lot of leverage. Usually on this type of amputation the kneecap was turned under to cover the end of the bone. This gave a good surface to bear weight while walking. However, in my case, I had no kneecap. They told me in England that there was too much gangrene gas in the area to do this. The patella had to go. This meant the plain end of my femur would have to do the job and bear the weight.

At the Prosthetic Clinic measurements were taken of my stump and my good leg to guide in the construction of the artificial leg. Over at one side was a large selection of various sizes of lower leg sections, from knee to ankle. They looked very much like the plastic milk bottles at carnivals that people try to knock off a shelf with a baseball. From this lineup the one closest to matching my remaining leg from calf and ankle was selected. The rest of the leg, foot, ankle and stump socket were made more or less custom. It took about a week before I returned for my final fitting, and then the leg was mine. It was not much to look at, not even skin toned, but it fit me and it worked.

When we were issued this not so beautiful leg, we were told that it was a temporary training leg just for us to learn to walk with. In four to six months, when our stump had been in use lifting this dead weight back and forth, it would reach its permanent shape or close to it. At this time, the GI issue would no longer fit properly and we could get a new one from any civilian limb maker we chose. This would be supervised and paid for by the Veterans Administration. Thus this first leg served its purpose as a trainer and a lot of money wasn't wasted on making it look good.

My next step was walking class. I believe this was part of the Physical Therapy Section. Here I got my first taste of "walking on the wood." After a PT person made sure I had the straps hooked up OK and my stump was in it properly, I took off, so to speak, down a narrow, wooden ramp with handrails on each side. It wasn't as easy as I thought it would be. It was kind of tricky trying to walk on this "stick" with a hinge in the middle. The hinge, artificial knee joint, bent just like a regular knee. However, unlike the one God designed for us, the man-made version could only take weight on it when it was fully extended. If the bottom part of the prosthesis wasn't all the way out, the knee joint would fold under you and down you would go.

The instructor told me to step out first with the artificial leg with a kicking motion of the stump. To step on it when it was straight and then bring my real leg through completed the step. This worked. I was walking, or at least moving on two legs again. I held the rails on each side of me and then I got myself going pretty good, so I let go and kept walking to the end of the ramp. I turned around and came back. It was a great feeling taking these first steps. They were jerky and terrible looking, but here I was walking on two legs again. While making these first steps I was kicking too hard and the instructor said, "Not so hard. You're not trying to kick field goals. Do it with a smoother motion." A few more times up and down the ramp, and I was walking with a much smoother gait. It would take a lot of practice before my walk would look near natural, but I knew I could do it.

Back on my ward at "The Glen," with the help of a cane, I continued to practice my walking. First I went back and forth in the ward then out into the hall and down to the men's room. Fellow patients gave me a smile and a, "Hello" and some even said, "Congratulation." One time I made a mistake and stepped off with my left foot. This is the way soldiers step off in the Army when marching. I let out a "Whoops," but I didn't take a nosedive onto the hard floor. Instead of falling, I quickly swung the artificial leg forward and thus kept my balance and completed my step. It worked great. I tried starting with my left, real leg, again and it worked great. It was much smoother and eliminated the jerk from my stride, so I kept on walking this way.

In the beginning most of us just used our new legs around the hospital. In the evening when we went into town, we parked the legs under our beds and took off on our crutches. Crutches were what we were used to, and we felt more confident on them. One could also move a lot faster. There came a time when this habit reversed itself. We had gotten used to the artificial legs, and many would not go off base if for some reason they could not wear theirs. I didn't move as fast on the leg, but I had my hands free when walking. It was also nice to look in the mirror and see myself in uniform standing there looking like a whole person. I got used to using my new leg faster than others and in a different way.

Shortly after I received my artificial leg, I was asked if I would go to Elizabeth City, N.C., to help with the Victory Bond Drive down there. As usual I said yes. It was fun, and I felt that I was still helping my country and the many wounded service men that the money from these bonds would help put back together. I had a room in a nice house in the suburbs of the city with some very nice people. The Bond people had arranged this. I had taxi service to the recruiting office and an Army car took me to speech locations, but after that I was on my own. One day I had finished my talks early in the afternoon and didn't want to go back to the house so soon. I asked my Army driver to let me off downtown, so I could take a look at Elizabeth City. He dropped me off, and since it was such a hot day a nice cold beer would taste good. Way down at the other end of the block I saw a sign that looked like it might belong to a place where I could get a cold one. I took another look and wondered if I had done the right thing. The block now looked mighty long and it was uphill too. I thought maybe I should hail a cab and head back to my quarters.

However I don't give up that easy. Sure it was a long walk, perhaps longer than I had ever made this wooden leg go. I stood there in the hot sun and thought. I had walked back and forth in the hospital corridors and around the ward many times during the day. Put that all together, and it was just about the same distance as the other end of the block. It was just all in a straight line and strange surrounding. I can do it. My confidence came back and off I went. The heat got to me a bit and I did a lot of sweating, but I made it and the cold beer tasted real good. This first walk down that street in Elizabeth City, N.C., did more to "rehabilitate" me than any other part of my rehab program. This is not a put down on my treatment at Walter Reed. They had made me well from being close to death and had given me the tools to work with. Putting this all together by myself here in North Carolina was the finale.

I remember the first intersection I came to. The light was against me, so I waited and wondered if I could make it across before it changed again. (This was always a problem.) Also, the curb I was headed for looked three feet high. Could I get up it? The light changed, and off I went holding my cane out for the right turning traffic to see so they wouldn't run me down. It worked, and they stopped to let me by. I had just arrived at the "cliff" on the other side of the street when the light turned green and the traffic started to roar at me. The curb was not so high close up, and I stepped up and out of the way just in time. I could feel the cars whooshing past the seat of my pants. The next time it was easier. However, I always had to be on the alert for those hurry-up drivers that counted on a pedestrian to take those last few steps at double speed because the leg only has one speed.

When I returned to the hospital, I was walking great and felt like an old pro. The artificial leg had become part of me, and I was walking very smoothly, at least on level ground. When the walking surface slants or becomes uneven, one really appreciates the wonderful knee joint and leg muscles that you were born with. There is no way you can walk and look good or normal with an artificial knee joint. It will not take up the slack, so walking along the side of a "hill," the wooden leg is either too short or too long according to which way you are walking. I soon got used to this and paid it no heed.

The rest of the summer went by quickly, highlighted by the surrender of Japan and the end of the war. I still went on talks in front of various organizations and groups explaining how money was still needed to rehabilitate the wounded that still were in our hospitals. The day after it was announced that the war was over, there was a sudden change in the attitude of the general public. Before when I stood at the bus stop in front of the hospital headed downtown, more than one car would almost instantly pull over and offer me a ride to wherever I was going. The day after the announcement, I waited 20 minutes as the cars streamed by. Finally someone who knew me stopped and offered me a lift.

In September I took a few days leave to join my parents in their fall visit to Atlantic City, N.J. Mom and dad had for some time taken a short fall and spring vacation at one of the ocean front hotels. I had been with them in '43 just prior to going on active duty and was looking forward to going again. Dad enjoyed the trip because he was born there and lived there until he was about eight years old, and mother liked to window ship at the many stores that lined that famous boardwalk. I just liked the whole place.

One evening when I was out on my own, I went into Silver Dollar Bar to have a beer and look around. It was a most interesting watering hole. The long bar top was covered with silver dollars. I was drinking my beer standing at the bar when a voice from the rear hollered, "Hey, Tiger." I knew it had to be someone from my division – The 10th Armored Tigers – and sure enough here came a second lieutenant, in uniform with a 10th Armored patch on his shoulder. He gave me a big handshake, and we started talking. It turned out that he was the sole survivor of an airplane crash that killed our entire division headquarters' staff, including our much admired commanding General "Pistol" Paul Newgarden. This happened as we were preparing to go overseas and delayed our crossing a month or two, so we missed D-Day. The lieutenant had just recently gotten out of the hospital and was eager to hear about his division in combat.

He also explained that he was here in Atlantic City as an escort for Miss America contestants and asked me to join him and them in the back room. I accepted, and he led the way to a nice, private dining room in the rear. It was a big room, for it held all 50 contestants, their escorts, the current Miss America and other officials. He said, "I'll introduce you to Miss America first." She was seated at the far end of the table, and as we approached she looked up and with a startled expression said, "Why, Don what are you doing here?" You should have seen the look on that lieutenant's face. Here was a PFC upstaging him, not intentionally, but upstaging nonetheless.

It was Venus Ramsey. She went to high school with me, but was one grade down. I remember that my cousin Joanne, who was in her class, had written me while I was in the hospital overseas and had mentioned that she had made Miss America. I replied with a big hello and belated congratulations. Man! Had that little schoolgirl grown up! Venus took over and introduced me to everyone and even added that she had had a crush on me. I wish I had know it back then, but it probably would not have made any difference, as I was in love and going steady with Joan McDonald.

Silver dollars were everywhere in the décor, and I told Venus how when I was wounded I had lost my good luck silver dollar that I had carried with me since I was 14 years old. My grandfather had given me a little bag full of them ever since I was born, and on my 14th birthday I put all but one in the bank. Someone mentioned how valuables disappeared in hospitals, taken by the workers. I said I don't think anyone took it for everything else that had been in my pockets, including a much prized hat insignia from an SS Troopers hat, was in a little bag beside me when I came to. I was wearing Australian Army pants with the watch pocket on the inner side of the waistband. That's where the dollar was. Our OD pants had the watch pocket on the outside so I think my lucky piece got incinerated with my bloody trousers.

One of the pageant officials announced it was curfew time, and everyone got up to leave. I shook hands with the lieutenant and wished him well. Out by the door, Miss America came over to me and kissed me on the cheek and handed me a silver dollar saying, "For good luck." I went back to the hotel feeling great. It was nice being kissed by Miss America even though she had been a year behind me at Coolidge High School. I also wondered how in the world I had overlooked such a beautiful girl.

The End of Army Life

B ack at the hospital things were beginning to wind down. The war had been over for about three months and there was no more demand for combat veterans to tell their story. The Victory Bond Drive was more or less a thing of the past, although they were still being sold. Banks, radio and other ads now did the selling. I began to start thinking seriously about my discharge. Although I spent a lot of time at home, I had had enough of hospital wards. My health was good and my prosthesis had become my best friend. I was about to ask my ward doctor about my discharge, when early one morning I was handed a sheet of paper with instructions. It was dated 5 December 1945.

There was no need to ask now. I was on my way out. On the top of the list was to report to the baggage room at Forest Glen to check baggage and "clothing equipment." That was easy. The only thing I had there was one uniform that I used when going on pass. What baggage an infantryman has – a duffel bag – had been captured or destroyed on the battlefield some place during the Battle of the Bulge. I didn't even have a uniform when I reached Walter Reed. The other items on the list for the 5th included reporting to the Red Cross, Social Service office, building 185. This I did, but also here there wasn't much for me to do. I was within three blocks of home and knew that I was going back to college in February, although I had not decided where as yet. However, to many, this office provided a lot of help during the transition from military to civilian life.

The next day I reported to Capt. Jones, the Separation Classification Officer. He would later supervise the signing of my discharge certificate. Everything was going smoothly until he discovered that I had not completed walking class. In fact I had only gone to two sessions. I couldn't be discharged without the head of walking class certifying that I could walk. So off I walked to the walking class and got the proper papers signed. They were very interested in my new way of walking: not kicking out with the artificial one, but stepping off with the good. I gave a small demonstration, and they nodded and mumbled and jotted down notes as I walked out the door.

Other stops on my checkout list included information and briefings on my pension rights, employment service and Civil Service as well as briefing on my GI Insurance options. Number nine, the last item on the list, went like this, "Report to the Detachment of patients Office for Discharge Certificate, Saturday, 8 Dec. 45. LEAVE THE HOSPITAL: SAT. 8 DEC 45." This I did and thus became a civilian again. It was a great occasion that I had been waiting for ever since I had been wounded. However, I was a bit sad too, for I truly like the Army – not the killing or bloody part – but the Army life in general. I had decided way back in basic training that at the end of the war I would go to West Point and become a career officer. Of course that was before I was wounded, and now I would be going to a civilian college.

I made my final salute to the officer of the day and walked into a different life, that of a one-legged man in a two-legged world. But, I knew I was going to do just fine.

IMPORTANT

NAME: Addor

YOU WILL PROBABLY BE DISCHARGED WITHIN THREE DAYS. DO NOT FAIL TO DO AS FOLLOWS:

1. Report to Supply Office or Baggage Room today to check baggage and clothing equipment.

    (A) If at Walter Reed, report at 1:00 PM to Supply Sergeant, Room #25, Patient Supply Office.

    (B) If at Forest Glen, report to Baggage Room, Forest Glen, immediately following admittance.

2. XX If at Walter Reed, report to Red Cross, Social Service Office between 1:00 and 4:00 PM.

3. XX If at Forest Glen, report at 1:30 PM to Room #1, Building #185, Forest Glen. **WED. 5 DEC. 45**

4. Report to Det. of Pts. Office, Walter Reed, at 8:30 AM, **THUR. 6 DEC. 45**
    (a) Capt. Jones, Separation Classification Officer.
    (b) Pension Claims.
    (c) United States Employment Service and Civil Service, Ward #21.

5. Report to Det. of Pts. Office, Walter Reed, at 9:00 AM, **FRI. 7 DEC. 45**
    (a) Capt. Jones, (signing of discharge certificate).
    (b) Insurance Office, Ward #21, at 10:00 AM.

6. If you have any personal problems, report to Personal Affairs Office, Walter Reed at 1:00 PM, **FRI. 7 DEC. 45**

7. All Ground Force Personnel must clear Ground Force Liaison Office prior to leaving Hospital.

8. If you are a member of the Army Air Corps, report to the Army Air Force Liaison Officer before leaving the hospital.

9. Report to Det. of Pts. Office for Discharge Certificate **SAT. 8 DEC. 45**

LEAVE THE HOSPITAL: **SAT. 8 DEC. 45**

Honorable Discharge

This is to certify that

DONALD J ADDOR 13 141 907 Private First Class

Company C 20th Armored Infantry Battalion

Army of the United States

is hereby Honorably Discharged from the military service of the United States of America.

This certificate is awarded as a testimonial of Honest and Faithful Service to this country.

Given at   Army Medical Center Washington D C

Date   8 December 1945

ROBT B SKINNER
Colonel Medical Corps
Asst Executive Officer

First Fire,
The Beginning of Combat

The 10th Armored Division left its assembly area on the Normandy Peninsula and headed inland to our first combat assignment. Newly arrived combat units were usually given a spot along the front lines that had little resistance left but still had pockets of the enemy to be cleared out. We had been assigned an area called Mars le Tour.

Our column rumbled through a section of Paris where many civilians lined the sides of the street waving and cheering and hollering for cigarettes and candy. If we had not seen road signs, we would not have known it was Paris as our route bypassed all of its famous landmarks. Our division, stretched out single file, made one hell of a long column. Someone said that if you stood in one spot along the way, it would take 24 hours to see it from nose to tail. We spent the night camped a few miles outside of the big city and could see it on the horizon. This was my first Paris experience. Even if we had been allowed to write home about it there was not much to tell.

The next morning we rolled on toward the frontline. I was riding in one of our 20th Armored Infantry ammo trucks and had a good view of the passing countryside. At first there were not many signs that a war had passed through this farmland. We saw farmers out plowing and around Cherbourg they teamed their horses single file. I saw as many as four of the big hairy-hoofed beasts pulling in a single line. The first signs of war were large burned out German vehicles that had been stripped down to the bare hulk.

As we traveled on, the enemy vehicles became more complete as they stood deserted by the side of the road and out across the fields. Then there were knocked out or disabled U.S. vehicles here and there. It sure gave me a funny feeling to see those machines just like in our column out there blasted away. Then came the trash and litter. It was everywhere: boxes, paper, cans, boards of all kinds and trash all over the area. What a mess, but the next sightings were much more shocking to the senses. Piles of German dead on each side of the road stacked like cord wood laying there all alone with a yellow tag on each toe – if they had any toes – waiting for a truck to come and pick them up. This was truly shocking but not as much as the first stack of dead GIs wearing the same uniform that I wore. I guess this was the first experience that brought home the fact that the war was for real, and I was in it.

We stopped for the night just short of the actual front. I was still with Battalion Headquarters, and it looked like I was here to stay. The Battalion Commander and his officers were looking at maps and other papers. Then the order was given to dismount and camp for the night. It seems that the town that was to be our base of operations was just down the road and our outfit was not due to move into it until tomorrow. I was looking for a place to roll out my sleeping bag when the Sarge told me to join a detail. This detail consisted of six men, including me. We were told to go ahead into the town and locate the three best buildings we could find and to secure them for Battalion Headquarters and two other command posts. There were only six of us and our only firepower was our M-1 rifles. We were worried, and the visions of those piles of dead were still fresh in our mind. We were told not to worry the town was empty and all we had to do was to make sure that none of the other units that were going to join us the next morning got the houses we picked.

Our little group headed down the road through the night, made darker by a heavy drizzle, with our fingers crossed. It was a spooky feeling being all alone in the dark with no sound at all except that of our shoes sloshing along. Suddenly the first buildings of the town loomed up before us. It was not much of a town, just a small village. Each side of the road was lined with old stone houses. Even in the dark we could see that most of them had been badly damaged by artillery sometime before our arrival. A few were just burned out stone shells. A guy who I shall call Joe and I were told to hold a house in pretty good shape for Battalion HQ. The others went to two houses across the street. Joe and I went into our house, and it was empty – no furniture, no nothing but broken window glass and rubble from shelling and shooting. But the roof was intact, and it was nice and dry. I took the first watch, and Joe found a spot to lie down and try and get some sleep.

I looked out the window and all was quiet. I tried to re-member what house the other guys were in but couldn't figure for sure. The drizzle had turned to a steady rain and played kind of a tune on the tile roof before it streamed down the front and made little rivers between the cobblestones. I had to shake my head to keep from dozing off. The sound of the rain and the quiet was getting to me. I looked over at Joe, and he was sound asleep in the corner in the back of the room with trash all around him. It was so quiet in the house and out there in the town that I wished something would liven things up a bit, like a stray cat, lost dog or horse. My wish was granted, but not in the way I had intended.

Down at the other end of the street I heard boots, lots of boots clashing against the cobblestones and then voices, Ger-man voices giving orders in harsh whispers. The sounds carried through the wet night air like they were right next door. I looked out the window and at the edge of town saw two large groups in the dark going into the first houses on each side of the street. I could hear them better now, and there was no doubt that they were the enemy. I couldn't tell how many, but to me it looked like the whole damn German army was moving into town. I called Joe in as loud a whisper as I dared. He popped right up. Boy, was I glad he was a light sleeper. We both watched out the window as they advanced. It wasn't an army but was a hell of a lot more than six M-1's could handle. This was our first time to see the real live enemy, but even a greenhorn could tell we were greatly outgunned.

As the patrol got closer it seemed to get larger and larger. I couldn't tell what the guys across the street were doing, but we had to do something soon. I asked Joe to check and see if there was a way out the back of this building. He went back and checked and returned quickly. He said yes there was a door leading outside, but it was so dark you couldn't see shit. I was about to say lets chance it. Maybe we could hide in the dark someplace out there until the rest of our outfit arrived. I was about to say this but all hell broke loose. The loudest machine gun chatter I had ever heard broke the silence and echoed through the wet night. At the same time an unholy horde of tracer bullets streaked passed our window and tore into the German patrol. I realized that these were .50-caliber guns and a lot of them. In seconds the enemy patrol was gone and all was quiet again until we heard the sound of tracks outside.

I looked out the door and saw two U.S. half-tracks moving into town. In their rear section each had a four barrel .50 caliber machine gun. A figure in one called out, "Anyone here!" I stepped out and introduced myself. The others came out also. We gathered around the guys who had saved our ass, and they said that they were from an anti-aircraft unit that was to be attached to the 20th AIB.

We went into the house and were just beginning to get acquainted when we heard a roar like a high-speed freight train passing overhead. Then there was an explosion that shook the whole town. The stone building shook, the ground shook, everything shook. Almost at the same time we exclaimed, "What the hell was that?" Instinctively we had flattened out on the floor. We were about to get up when we heard another great roar approaching. This time it hit closer. Across the street a couple of the stone houses were blown completely away. Nothing was left but a gigantic hole. A couple more of these huge artillery shells roared in but hit further away. Even our battle-experienced AA comrades said that they had never seen or heard anything like it before.

By this time the night was nearly done and the major would be coming to set up his new Headquarters in this building. We sat down and leaned back against the wall to rest a bit wondering what might happen next. For an empty town in the dead zone, it sure had been active. I opened a box of K-rations and munched them down wishing I had something hot and better tasting to eat. However, it was something to eat and it stopped my stomach's hunger calls. I guess I fell asleep as the next thing I knew the town was full of our guys. I jumped up as the Sarge came in, and he said the major liked the place and to get busy setting up the switchboard and other HQ gear.

The corporal who had been in charge of our last night's detail was trying to tell the lieutenant about the German patrol and the heavy shelling. I went over to back his statement up, but we got nowhere. The lieutenant and Sarge too, just laughed at us and said we had just been lonely and scared and had imagined it all. I pointed to the big hole across the street, but it was shrugged off as old stuff. After all, the Division had been informed that this was a dead town and a section of the front with little or no action. I went back to bringing in more items to set up our Battalion HQ and said to the corporal, "Well we tried to warn them!"

I was headed out to the street again and the Sarge was just ahead of me. As we stepped out onto the street, we both heard a swish and a German mortar shell hit about three feet in front of us. It whacked the cobblestones and bounced a couple of times then lay there right in front of us. It did not explode. It was a dud! We ducked back into the house as three more shells whooshed in. These were not duds and sent shrapnel flying across the street, but no one was hit. The Sarge looked at me and said, "Shit," and asked me to tell him again what happened last night.

Now the mortar is a foot soldier's weapon and the size of the shells indicated that the enemy was not too damn far away.

Not exactly, but close to it. This four-barrel anti-aircraft unit is mounted on a trailer. The ones that came to our rescue at Mars La Tour were mounted on half-tracks.

Below: This is an example of a big German railroad gun, but it is not nearly as big as the one that shelled us during our "first combat."

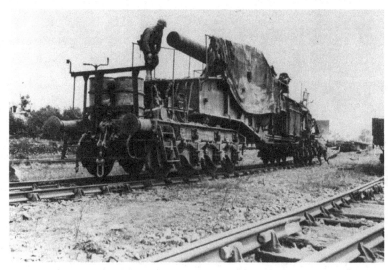

All during the day we received shelling both from mortar and artillery, but no shelling from that really big gun. During one of these mortar attacks I was at the back of our building where the bathroom facilities had been dug. Since two guys were already straddling the slit trench. I decided to relieve myself over against the side of a shed.

I had just begun when three rounds of mortar fire came whistling in. They hit very close in a cabbage patch a few yards away. What a mess. Dirt, mud and cabbages flew everywhere. I cut my relief job short right then and hit the ground. One guy was able to make it off the slit trench running for cover with his pants around his ankles. The other was not so lucky. He fell into the slit trench, splashing in the mess below. He climbed out, pulled up his pants and went off somewhere. I always wondered where and how he got himself cleaned up, for he could not have stayed the way he was. The enemy could have smelled him coming a mile away. Safe inside when the tale was told everyone had a big laugh. I thought later, it was a funny thing to laugh about. A little bit closer or if those shells had hit on hard ground, we all could have been killed. It was funny the things we sometimes laughed at in combat.

We had several more mortar attacks during the day, but none came as close, at least to me and Battalion Headquarters, as the ones that blew up the cabbage patch and the dud that almost landed on top of Sarge. The information on the direction of the attack was passed on to B Company and they sent patrols out to try and find them. I don't know if they were able to locate that German patrol, but they never attacked us again. That night the artillery started to shell us. First it was the "88's" and then we heard the roar of the freight train, and the whole town shook as one of those huge shells hit just behind the houses across the street.

The Sarge, the lieutenant and the major all rushed into the front room shouting, "What the hell is that?" I hate to be an "I told you so," but I told them that's what I tried to tell them about our first (last night's) stay. They didn't laugh now but hit the floor as another big shell roared in. This one went over the town and blew a big hole in a cow pasture. We kept hugging the floor and waiting as one more could be heard approaching. It also did not hit in the town, but shook it good and proper. When morning came patrols were sent out trying to find some clue as to the location of this monster. Some of our artillery guys tried to figure the direction by studying the huge craters. They got the general direction, but that's all. An artillery piece that big could be firing from over twenty miles away.

The next day a big search was begun trying to locate that big artillery piece. Even an artillery spotter in "Piper Cub" airplane joined in the hunt, but not a trace of it or its crew could be found. That night four more of those big shells came roaring into town. No great damage was done as they only hit close, but even so these big blasts were most disconcerting. If they did hit in our center there would not be much left of our outfit. Before the night was over everyone was ordered to pull out of town, and we spent the rest of the night in the hills overlooking the town.

This went on for several days. We worked in the town during the day and pulled out at night. We watched the shelling and moved back into our Headquarters building during the daylight hours. This was annoying, but safe. The Germans never did catch on. One day when I was working my shift on the Headquarters switchboard a runner from C Company dashed in shouting, "We saw the son-of-a-bitch. We saw it!" It seems his detail was scanning a town across the river when they saw a huge artillery piece on a railroad car being rolled from one building to another. Yes, they had the coordinates of the building and the gun was still in it. The lieutenant took the directions into the major's office. Soon the switchboard was busy. A little while later we saw a group of our bombers fly overheard and heard them blast that building into rubble and "Big Bertha" with it. Later our unit was informed that the Allies had been looking for the big gun for sometime, as it was the last of the giant German railroad guns. We were given credit for destroying it along with many thanks.

In a few days our tour of duty on the "quiet front" ended, and we moved off to Luxembourg where we gathered to cross the Moselle River and spearhead the Moselle-Saar Valley drive for Patton's Third Army.

HOW DIRTY CAN YOU GET
AND A LONELY SONG

One thing for sure with the infantry in combat is that you do not have the comforts or conveniences of home or even an Army barracks. Fighting a war on the ground is a dirty job. You are constantly in mud, smoke and greasy or sooty equipment. It would be nice to have at least one bath a day, but Jim and I had not had one for two months. This was not entirely the Army's fault. They tried to keep us clean by sending portable shower tents to our units whenever possible. However, with schedule of towns to take and ground to cover that General Patton set for our 10th Armored Division it was hard to get these shower units to us. Also there are no referees to blow a whistle to stop the action or halftimes to take a bath.

Those showers had visited the 20th AIB several times, but each time Jim and I had been away working some detail. I guess the word got around or maybe we smelled so strong that our CO thought the enemy could detect us. Anyhow, one morning when we reported to headquarters, we were told to take a vehicle and go on back to Thionville and get a bath, but hurry on back as soon as it was done. There was a rather nice but very muddy Mercedes at the motor pool. It had been "captured" a while back and was used as an unofficial Army vehicle when needed. We were told to take it for the unofficial trip back to Thionville. This was more than OK with us as this vehicle was usually just for officers. We took off down the muddy road where a battered sign pointed to the location for our scrub down as well as other towns we had recently chased the Germans out of. The car just hummed along and Jim cussed at the six or more inches of mud dropped on the hardtop by trucks and tank tracks. He said to me that he sure would like to be able to see what she would do on a clear road. It had been raining as usual, but after a while the rain stopped. That made driving a lot easier and pretty soon we saw a roadblock up ahead. As we slowed down an MP waved us over to the side of the road. I got out and followed the MP over to a shack that they were using as an office.

I was asked where we were going and why. He asked for official orders. I told him that our CO, Maj. Desobry, had said we smelled bad and to go into Thionville and get a bath, and that's what we were trying to do. I showed him my dog tags but had no other identification on me except a letter from home. I seemed to have him convinced. It did not take any brains to see we needed a bath. I had noticed that the MP officer behind the desk was eyeballing that Mercedes and seemed to be drooling. Another MP had checked out Jim in the car. Everything seemed to be OK then the officer said that we could go ahead if we wanted, but the Mercedes had to stay. This was the end of the front lines, and it was not a registered Army vehicle. He would have to impound it! Regulations! Jim was close enough to hear what he said. He got out of the car and walked over to me. As he did the Mercedes began to roll. It rolled off the side of the road, past the beginning of the bridge and plunged into the Moselle River. Jim said, "Shit! The hand break didn't work."

The MP's had run over to see where it had gone, and we hitched a ride back toward the front where we had come from. At the motor pool, we told them what had happened. They felt bad about loosing such an interesting vehicle but realized someone should have known better than to have sent it out of our area. We were issued an official U.S. Army Jeep complete with machine gun on a pole behind the front seats. It was a

.30-caliber air-cooled with a belt of ammo hanging out already for action. This is how most of our Jeeps looked. When we got back to the bridge and the end of the front lines another shift of MP's was on. I waved a piece of paper at them, and they waved us on into Thionville. We were official and looked the part.

We entered the town and what a shock. This sure was "behind" the lines. Everything was spit and polish. Troops were marching this way and that, in formation and counting cadence. They were even wearing neckties! There was an officer standing nearby fully attired for a dress parade. We motored over and asked him where we could get a bath. We didn't have to say anymore. One look and it was obvious that we were combat infantry from up front. He pointed down the street to a building and said that was the public bath and that the Army had taken it over. By now we had attracted a good bit of attention, and a group of these well-dressed soldiers crowded around gawking at us. We felt like we were from another planet, and we looked like it too.

The officer looked at the machine gun and our side arms, I had my M-1 that I had been issued back in the states even though my present job called for a carbine. We were informed that live ammunition was against regulations back here. I told him where we were from it was a damn necessity and we were going back right after we got cleaned up. He told us to park the Jeep over by the Headquarters building, and it and the ammo would be safe.

As we were about to leave, I noticed a green, brown and white stripped ribbon his uniform next to a good conduct one. I asked him what it was. He kind of puffed up and said, "That's the European Theater of Operations Ribbon!" Oh! I said, and we went and parked the Jeep. We had been fighting in the ETO for more than three months, but that was the first I had ever heard of it. About a week later we were issued an ETO ribbon at mail call.

As we walked down the street towards the bathhouse, we couldn't help but notice how things had changed since we had last been in Thionville. It had been a muddy, shell-blasted city. But now the streets had been cleaned, and most of the buildings had been or were being repaired. I wondered where all the glass had come from, for there had not been an unbroken windowpane in the whole town. We arrived at the bathhouse, and it was a busy place. We sure weren't the only ones in need of a bath. A GI took our names and asked if we wanted a shower or bathtub. I took the tub as I had not been in or seen one since I had been home on leave a year ago. We were informed that there would be about an hour and a half wait for us.

We went outside and stood there wondering where to go and what to do. I was watching a group of civilians across the street repairing a building that had been damaged by artillery fire. A lot of work had been done since we blew through here. It was nice to see a town getting back to "normal" so soon. There were also a lot of happy looking civilians going about their business. What a contrast to the way the towns across the bridge and not too many miles down the road looked. Here comes another group of fresh new soldiers marching by in cadence. As they were passing, the officer in charge took a good look at us and asked us to join them. They were going to a USO show. It sounded like a good thing to do, so we went along but not in step. Neither of us had seen a USO show. This was about as close to the front as they were allowed to get. Up there we did not have the time or place for these kind of goodies. I guess Patton would have said something like, "You can't win a war sitting on your ass watching a show."

The troops were halted in front of a building that had seen better days. It was an old theater that had been patched here and there with whatever was available. Pieces of old "Hiel Hitler" type posters still clung to the walls inside and out. It was a rustic old place that the ravages of war had not entirely been cleaned away. It made us feel at home. The troops filed in taking seats downstairs. We chose to go up in the balcony where there were fewer GI's, and our appearance and smell would be less offensive. We sat near to the end of the isle so we could leave early if we had to. Looking down on all of the "olive drab" seated below, I noticed there were others that showed the signs of combat experience and were back here on R and R.

The old theatre was really something to behold. There were still some holes in the upper walls and roof, and daylight could be seen. It was like a Hollywood set, but this was the real thing. I wondered about how many years people had performed on the stage below. A couple of hundred at least. The band interrupted my thoughts. Then a man in a tuxedo came out and said a few words and cracked some corny jokes. He introduced some lady, but I didn't catch her name. The lights went out and then a spotlight came on encircling a beautiful lady in a long shimmering evening gown. What a sight. Most of us had not seen any woman for almost a year, and all of a sudden here was this beauty.

She started to sing in a soft mellow voice. Soft but could easily be heard throughout the old hall. The song was "I'll Walk Alone." The words went something like this: "I'll walk alone because to tell you the truth. I'm lonely..." It almost stopped my heart. I had not heard it before. Even Axis Sally had not played this lonely song to us. When the song ended she waited for the applause but none came. I could see the disappointment in her young face, but as she started to walk off stage the building exploded with the clapping of hands. It went on and on, and I added mine. Now she was smiling and bowing as the applause continued. Her great performance had taken us all back across the Atlantic to where ever we came from in the states. It had taken a while to come out of the trance and back to reality.

I don't remember what else happened, only that song. We had to leave for our bath and slipped out shortly after her song. The rest of the show would have been an anticlimax anyhow. Back at the bathhouse I was escorted to a shiny, white tiled room with a big tub in the center. What a wonderful feeling to soak and scrub all of that grime off of my body. I soaked there for as long as I dared. They set no time limit, but we did have to get back to our outfit. The only unpleasant part was that I had no clean uniform and had to put the dirty one back on, but at least I was clean. Jim and I got back to the motor pool at Battalion Headquarters without event. Not even a sniper to deal with. Jim went back to his job with the welding torch, and I went and reported into the major's office. That song was still running through my head, and when I finally got to go to "bed" I looked at the photo of Joan that I kept in the webbing of my helmet liner and wondered if she was as lonely as I was. It had been a good day! I was clean. No one had shot at me, and there had been no shells to dodge. I fell asleep with visions of that beautiful singer and her song in my head.

WE RUN OUT OF TANK AMMO

It was in Alsace-Lorraine, maybe just after we had crossed into Germany that we hit stiff resistance when trying to take a fairly large town from the enemy. They were holding tight, and we couldn't get even one foot into that town. I was with Headquarters of the 20th Armored Infantry Battalion of the 10th Armored Division, and we were spearheading the Moselle-Saar Valley Drive for Patton's Third Army.

Temporary Headquarters had been set up in a field about a mile out of town. We had hoped to be better quartered inside a warm and dry building by now, but in spite of the shelling being given by our tanks, the Germans were still there. The major had called for an air strike, but although it was not raining where we were, it was still too overcast for the flyboys to help us. It was evening, and we were sitting around a fire made of ammo boxes and trash when things got worse. The tanks had run out of ammunition just when they were making progress.

A call was made to Battalion supply, but they had not received any from Division. It went up the chain of command, but no one had any shells for our tanks or tank destroyers. This had happened once before with gasoline, and we had taken a beating with many casualties. We assumed a bridge had washed out, as Patton's Red Ball Express was doing a great job. We found out later that on both cases our supply was stopped by High Command to slow Patton down to keep the British from looking bad.

The tank commander, who had brought the request for more ammo, said he didn't need a whole lot, just enough to stop any German counter attack and to maybe bluff his way into town. We were all sitting around the fire cursing the enemy, cursing the lack of shells to fight with and cursing most everything else. Suddenly I got an idea. It was like this: when tanks moved from one firing position to another they only took the "clover leave" boxes with them. Any loose rounds were left behind to be salvaged by the next group that moved into the area. This would mean three or four rounds at every spot our tanks had stopped to give "artillery" support to the infantry. The major and tank officer agreed that it was a good idea, and I was ordered to round up a detail to do it.

The tank officer gave me a general idea of where to look. We left at dawn with a supply truck pulling an ammo trailer. The actual finding of shells turned out to be easier than expected, but the breaking of the truck's mud chain held us up. When we hit sections of the road that were not covered by a foot of mud a link would break, and a section of the chain would make a racket slapping against the wheel well. This didn't bother our ears too much, but it alerted snipers way before the normal engine noise of the truck. The broken chain made enough noise that even a deaf sniper could have heard us coming. We were hunting for shells just a couple of miles behind the actual fighting. This was an area not yet cleared of snipers or small pockets of resistance. These would be cleared by whatever foot infantry unit was assigned to mop up behind our spearhead.

We drew some sniper fire, but aside from a few more holes in the truck no damage was done. At our last stop we picked up six loose rounds. We also gathered some wood from the broken up shell container for the fire back at Headquarters. The cloverleaf shape came from the round cardboard tubes that housed each shell for delivery. The tubes were in groups of three with six of them held in a wooden frame of a box. We also took a good number of these heavy cardboard tubes to feed the flames back at HQ. We turned back to head home feeling that our trip had been a success. We had recovered a lot more shells then we had expected. We didn't take the same road back, as our map showed us a shorter return route. We were also in a hurry to get these shells to the tanks waiting for them.

As we approached a small crossroads town, I noticed that vehicles had started to pull over to the side of the road for a good distance. We were in a hurry and sped on through the intersection without thinking. A Jeep with a driver and an officer followed close behind us. Now we should have known what was going on and why we should have stopped. The Germans had an odd way of shelling us. They shelled certain intersections and areas where they thought we might be. They did this in an exact military manner. By the book, or I should say manual. At a certain time they sent a certain amount of 88's at a target. It was always the same. So troops in the area checked their watches, and if it was close to shelling time stopped, waited, counted the blasts and then drove on through.

This we didn't do, and we ran right into the center of the shelling. When the first shell hit the road right in front of us the driver pulled to a stop by a stone wall, and we got the hell out of the truck in a hurry. Tank ammo is pretty stable, but a hit from an 88 would blow it sky high. Across the road was a nice solid stone house. In the front doorway a man was waving us over. I was crouched down by the stone wall when the next shell hit. Shrapnel spewed all around. A piece hit the stone wall right in front of me. So close that stone dust was blown in to my eyes blurring my vision for a second.

Now was the time to get the hell across the street and into that house. As I dashed toward the beckoning man, another shell hit the street almost on top of me. I was not hit at all. Out of the corner of my eye I saw that the officer from the Jeep that had been behind us was not so lucky. He was also heading to the house. A piece of the shrapnel had caught him in the face. He went down with blood spewing all over the place. I thought his head had been blown away.

As we entered the house I looked back and that officer was lying there in a pool of blood. He sure looked dead. The elderly man was shouting French at us and waving his hands around pointing to thick walls that were hundreds of years old. He led us to the basement patting the wall again and again to assure us how safe it was.

The basement was a safe place for sure. The ancient walls made a perfect bomb shelter. We could hear the explosions and feel the ground shake, but we were secure. Beside the guys from our truck there was the Jeep driver, another soldier and a couple of civilians. Our French host had gone some place upstairs. However, he soon was at the top of the basement steps waving his arms and hollering at us in French. I knew a little French and gathered that there was something he wanted one of us to see up there.

I went up the steps, and he led me down the hall to the front door that was standing open. He pointed to the street, and there was the officer that I had thought was dead, staggering around in the middle of the shelling. His face was all bloody, and he couldn't see where he was or where he was going. I said, "Oh Shit!" and dashed out to him. He was a bloody mess but was able to follow me back to the house. We did not waste anytime. Although the shelling had moved down the street, a bit of those 88's were still too damn close for comfort. Back in the house the Jeep driver had figured out what was going on, and he was there to lead his officer to the safety of the basement.

We had just gotten him laid down as comfortable as possible when the French man's wife was standing by us with a bowl of hot water and clean towels. They washed his face and things were not as bad as it had looked when I saw that shrapnel knocked him down in the street. A piece of jagged metal had torn off part of his nose, and he was missing one of his eyes, but when the blood was washed away the other eye was OK. The bleeding was stopped and the corporal had taken a bandage out of his first aid kit. The only way to get it to cover the damaged flesh was to wrap it around the damaged area, covering his nose and both eyes.

The shelling was over, and as we prepared to leave and start our trip back to the front, I asked the driver where he had been going. He said he was taking the lieutenant up to the front as a replacement. He added that they had passed an aid station back down the road a couple of miles, and he would deliver the officer there instead. With that I thanked the French couple in the best French I knew. As we pulled away I could see them waving at us until they were out of sight.

The rest of the return trip was uneventful. We didn't even get lost after it got dark. The driver pulled the truck over to the side of the road as much as possible when we arrived at Battalion Headquarters. The major and tank officer were pleased with the load of shells we had retrieved. The driver was told to get that truck into the town as soon as possible. The driver argued that the truck and trailer were way too big for the small muddy road at night and through woods that had not been completely cleared of the enemy. We should make the delivery with a half-track! I agreed, but that didn't count for much as we were ordered to proceed with the truck.

The road into the town was barely two lanes wide for small cars. The surface had been black hard topped, but the heavy Army vehicles hard cut through this some time back, and now it was a muddy mess. Although it was not raining, visibility was very poor. It was a dark night with no moon or stars. Of course this close to the enemy we could not use any headlights, not even the "cat-eyes." The truck moved slowly down a hill and into the woods. We crossed a small creek that was piped under the road. It was mushy, but passable. Now we went up a hill where in about a half mile the woods would end and then down into the town.

We were not too far up the hill when we met an infantry patrol. They told us to stop and go back because a large German patrol was in front of us. It was no place for a big truck hindered by a heavy trailer. Now the problem was how to turn around on this narrow road. The patrol helped unhitch the trailer and swing it around while the driver wiggled the truck back and forth to get it pointed in the right direction. During all of this time we could hear the German patrol off in the woods ahead of us. It seemed like they might catch up with us and open fire at any minute.

We got through the creek area again, but the pipe had been crushed and the road bed was changing into a mud bed. Back at Battalion Headquarters we explained what had happened and again asked to use a half-track. There was one sitting nearby. This time they loaded the tank shells into a Jeep. It was too big a load for that little vehicle, and it had not gone more than a few yards when it sank into the soft ground up to its frame. Now we got the half-track, but had lost a lot of valuable time.

As we headed toward the wooded section of the road, dawn was breaking. This made it easier to see where we were going, but it also made it easier for the enemy to see us. When we arrived at the creek, we found that it had been churned into a real mud bog. A truck before us had just barely made it through the mess. The driver hesitated but went ahead into the mire. We had no choice but to give it a try. These shells had to get there and soon. We got about halfway across, and down she went to almost above the tracks. Now a half-track has a lot of power, but the engines just roared and roared. We didn't move an inch.

I got out on the hood and slid down the front of the vehicle to the bumper and winch. Maybe we could get out with the help of the winch. I'd winched Jeeps out of similar situations many times, but this wasn't a Jeep. Besides there wasn't a big enough tree anywhere near the other side. I was sitting there wondering what to do and maybe I said a little prayer for a Sherman tank appeared just where we needed it.

I got the winch loose and the cable across the mud to the tank, and with the winch reeling in and the Sherman backing up we were out of there in no time. That muddy mess had caused quite a traffic jam on the far side. As we headed away I saw another half-track get stuck. Now a truck or half-track spinning wheels in mud makes a lot of noise, and lots of vehicle noise attracts enemy artillery so we moved on out as fast as we could. We had just about reached the edge of the woods when we heard the 88's screaming overhead heading for that muddy-troubled spot.

The driver halted the half-track at the edge of the woods, and what we saw ahead of us was not a pleasant sight. From here to the village was open country. Not even a tree. It was also a pretty steep downgrade. The worst sight was all of the vehicles, our vehicles, which had been knocked out in the road and on each side. This meant that the German had this area zeroed in and under surveillance. This was not a good situation. The question was how to get from the edge of the woods to the town below where the road ended in a T-junction.

A mad dash was the only way and a heavy half-track was neither fast nor very maneuverable. I was standing up in the front seat through the ring mount of the .50-caliber machine gun. I pulled the bolt back to full load the weapon and asked the driver what he thought. He said he thought we could make it down to the town ahead of any enemy fire. His biggest concern was a burned out truck sat right in the middle of the road. He said, "Just hope the ground at the edge of the road is not too soft." If it were the half-track would roll over before he could swing it back onto the road.

We crossed our fingers, so to speak, and I manned the "50," ready to fire if fired upon. Down the hill we went faster than I thought one of the heavy vehicles could go. The driver swung around the truck in the center of the road. Our crossed fingers worked. The ground held. As we entered the town with all brakes locked, the enemy artillery blasted the road where we had been seconds before. At the speed we were going even with the brakes on, the track was going too fast to make the turn. We held on tight and crashed into the stone wall. What an entrance.

As we caught our breath and recovered form our violent entry, an officer came running up to us. He wanted to know what the hell was going on. We did look odd sitting there with the front half of our vehicle buried in the wall while dust and stones came raining down. I told him this was the tank ammo that someone wanted. He told me to take it over there, pointing down the road to the left. I answered with a polite, "Sorry Sir, orders were to deliver it to the town. It's yours now!" I jumped out of the half-track and started to run back up the hill and back to Battalion Headquarters. I don't remember if I told him I had been up over 26 hours getting those shells to him or not. I was so tired I didn't really care. I made it across that no man's land without being shot at. Apparently one GI wasn't worth the effort, although I did keep those dead vehicles between the Germans and me as much as possible. I am also a pretty fast runner especially when my ass is in danger.

Back up the hill with all the woods around me I felt pretty safe and relaxed a bit. The first time I was able to do this in some time. The shelling that had been going overhead had stopped. The sun had come out, a rare event in itself, and I was heading back to get something to eat and hopefully some sleep. At least a little bit of it. When I got to the creek, or where it had been, a sad sight confronted me. A half-track was sunk in the middle of the mire up to its mine rack on the driver's side. Around it were at least four bodies and three others were laying or sitting at the edge of the road. All badly wounded. I asked if I could help and was informed that the medics were on the way.

We had gotten out of there just in time. I continued on the way to where I was going. I came out of the woods and could see my destination not too far ahead. I heard and saw an airplane circle overhead and head back toward the town. I looked to my right and saw some GI waving at me from his foxhole. I waved back to him, but he waved and waved and pointed skyward. At about the same time I looked up, I heard the whistling scream of a bomb. There it was a little black spot right above me coming down fast. I dove into a water-filled rut and looked up. That spot was getting bigger and bigger and looked like it was going to land right on top of me. Then suddenly it seemed like it took a right-hand turn, and it hit in a ravine about 50 feet off the road.

It just blew a lot of mud all over the place, but it was a blood chilling experience that I'll never forget. I was damn glad that was the only bomb I had any close experience with. It was one of ours. It had stuck when it should have dropped on the town. The pilot came back to check on us. We waved our thanks, trying to say everything was OK. He wiggled his wings and flew off to where ever he came from.

I reported back to the CO (Commanding Officer) that the mission had been accomplished. The tank ammo delivered. He looked at my puffy eyes and me and said, "You better go get some sleep, but first go to the aid station. You got a cut on your face." I didn't need anyone to tell me I needed to sleep. It had been more than 24 hours since I had had any sack time. I was almost out on my feet. So tired I didn't even realize my cheek had been cut. Must have been that shell blast by the wall that blew rock in my face.

The medics were only a short walk from where I was. When I got there a medic washed the area with alcohol and put some medication on it. I told him I didn't want any bandage on it, as it wasn't much more than a scratch. He then asked me if wanted to be put in for a Purple Heart. He shoved some forms at me. I shook my head and said no, it wasn't really a wound. He claimed it was good enough for the medal, but I still refused. This was not so much for myself, but I could picture my mother getting word that I had received the Purple Heart for being wounded in action, and it would really shake her up. I turned down another one for a cut on my hand from a piece of shrapnel for the same reason. This was just before they started to give points toward going home and Purple Hearts counted high.

I headed back to my half-track and found a fairly dry place for my bedroll and got ready to try to get some sleep. I looked down at myself and boy, was I a mess. Covered with mud, rock dust and blood from the wounded officer. I needed a good hot bath, clean cloths and a steak dinner. This was all in the land of wishful thinking. No such thing for the infantry, particularly at the front. So I chewed up a box of cold K-rations and flopped down. As I drifted off to sleep, I dreamed about soaking in a hot tub while eating a big, juicy steak.

When I woke up the next day, I was told that our planes had bombed the town and chased the Germans out. Battalion Headquarters was now in a large department store in the town and, oh yes, they had not needed the tank ammunition after all. The French would have said, "C'estla guerre," but I think I said shit!

WE SET UP SHOP DOWN TOWN

Those fighter-bombers had done a good job, and our infantry and tanks were able to run the Germans out of the town. Battalion Headquarters moved in and set up on the first floor and basement of a large department store that was still in pretty good shape with only a few holes in it here and there. The best thing about it was that it was warm and dry. We had a real roof over our heads for a change. To make things even better our chow truck had caught up with us, and we were going to have hot meals at least for a while.

Chow call was sounded, and we were ready to go for it. It was then we realized that we had been eating out of C-ration cans and K-ration boxes for so long most of us did not know where our mess kits had gotten. I know mine had been flattened when a case of ammo had fallen on it. That had been some time back, but this was the first time I had had a need for it. Our need was filled when one of the guys found the china department in our store.

We helped ourselves to the largest china plates we could fine. It was like back home. We took our pretty civilian style plates to the chow line, and you should have seen the expressions on the servers' faces when we held the plates out to be served. Not only were they prettier than the GI mess kits, but also there was more room for more food on them. We were the envy of all who ate at that chow line that day. We had another break at least while the food was being served. The rain let up, and we were able to eat our food without it being diluted and chilled by rainwater. When we were through, we just tossed the plates against a pile of rubble and calmly walked back to headquarters.

We got new plates for the next chow call and did the same for each meal as long as we were in this town and that department store. The Germans had been driven out of the city, but they were still giving stiff resistance in the countryside a few miles past the edge of town. We also began to receive a lot of artillery fire. We were glad we had our cellar for protection when it got heavy. I was informed that I was assigned to switchboard duty for the night and that an important patrol was being sent out to gather information on what lay ahead in the way of terrain and what the enemy had out there.

The patrol started out soon after dark. As usual they laid telephone line out behind them as they proceeded into the darkness. We had radio sets that could have been used, but we never did, as it was too easy for the Germans to intercept radio messages even though we had a secret "crystal" for each day. A telephone line had to be spliced in order to hear any messages and that was not easy to do without detection. Rolling miles of wire out was not easy, but much more secure. I sat down at the switchboard to begin a long wait for a call-in progress report. Calling them was forbidden as the enemy could hear the ring, and the whole patrol could be detected and wiped out. A patrol like this one was to gather information, not engage the enemy.

Time went by quickly at first, but then began to drag as no calls came in. The patrol leader was supposed to check in at least every half hour, but more than two hours had gone by without even one little tingle on the switchboard. I stared hard at it but that didn't help. The lieutenant from the major's office kept popping in for some kind of message for our commander. We were all getting nervous wondering what could have gone wrong. The distant rumble of heavy artillery fire did nothing to calm us. We just had to sit and wait and hope that the lack of check-ins only meant some mechanical problem or that the enemy was too close at hand to risk a telephone call.

A guy named Joe said he would take over the watching for a while as I was getting kind of cramped up. I found a place to sit down at the far end of the room near the other light bulb hanging from the ceiling. I couldn't nap or rest, so I decided it would be a good time to write a short note home to my mom and dad. I was in luck. I still had an envelope and a sheet of paper in the web of my helmet liner. Finding paper and envelopes had been a problem at first, as one just doesn't find those things in a combat zone. I had even written a letter on the back of a piece of wallpaper I had stripped off a wall in some French town. I got the idea to ask mom to send an envelope and paper in each letter she wrote. Now I had a regular supply. It didn't take long as there was not much of anything I could say. We couldn't mention anything about where we were or even the weather. I couldn't' understand the latter. I think the Germans had a better idea of what the weather was like that I did. They were never more than a mile away, and we shared the same miserable rain and drizzle. However, just hearing that I was OK was plenty of comfort to them.

It was now approaching dawn and still not a word. We were really worried. In fact the lieutenant has stopped running back and forth and was sitting on the floor near the door. A report had come in from the outpost that they had heard a lot of artillery and small arms fire out in the direction the patrol had gone. We were about to give them up for being lost, killed or captured. When the officer in command of the patrol stumbled through the door. He was muddy, tired and ugly looking, but he was smiling from ear to ear. The lieutenant jumped up and led him to the major' office before he could even say hello.

It turned out that they had run into plenty of enemy and artillery fire. In fact it was so heavy that it kept cutting the telephone line running along the ground. They had spliced it at least fifteen times then had to give up. But no one had been hurt, and a lot of useful information had been obtained. Well I guess you could say all's well that ends well, but that was sure one hell of a wait but better than being on the other end of the line.

I Learn How I Got
Out of Bastogne

Until the summer of 1948, I still had no idea how I got out of Bastogne when the Germans surrounded it. In the summer of '48 I was on vacation in Mexico with my good friend Hank Dierkoph. We were at the Floating Gardens of Xochimilco near Mexico City waiting our turn for a boat ride. It was very hot and I didn't know how much walking I might have to do, so I had left my artificial leg back at the hotel and was using a pair of German style cane crutches. Out of the waiting crowd a gentleman walked over to us and said hello.

He asked me if I minded if he asked how I had lost my leg. I was about to say no when he asked if it was in the Army. Of course I said yes. He asked where. When I said outside of Bastogne, Belgium, his eyes lit up and he said, "I was the Battalion Surgeon for the 20th Armored Infantry Battalion. I was there too." As we talked it turned out that he was the doctor who had taken care of me in that basement aid station. He said he remembered me because I was one of those he had put into ambulances with hopes that the Germans would have mercy and let the wounded through their lines to better medical care. He had picked the wounded that he knew would not survive if they did not get better medical care than what he could give.

He said that he had seen to it that the ambulances were well marked on all sides when they went off into the fog. That was the last he ever saw or heard of them. I told him I had been wondering all this time about how I got out of that surrounded city. I told him about how I had reached the hospital in Paris on

Christmas Eve and how the gangrene was so bad that they had to amputate my leg. He said he was afraid that would happen and that he was sorry. I told him that it had saved my life, and I was doing great and attending the University of Maryland. Since he was a doctor I added that I usually wore an artificial let and did right well on it. He was pleased to hear that.

As we parted to get our boats for our ride through the floating gardens, he said, " I have worried about those ambulances all of these years. I wondered if they got through or whether the Germans killed everyone like they did in some places around Bastogne, or if my patients had been taken prisoner." We both agreed that it was a strange coincidence and perhaps a bit of a miracle that we should meet on this hot day way down in Mexico. Sometimes it is a small world!

We Met Again Far From Bastogne

An interesting happening that went back to my being wounded and trying to get back into Bastogne, Belgium, occurred while I was working as a Public Information Officer at Walter Reed Army Medical Center in 1952. Yes, back where I had been a patient during World War II. Now we were fighting a war in Korea, and the hospital was once again filled with combat wounded.

Early one morning I received a call from a civic organization that wanted a speaker for a dinner that same evening – a soldier that had been in combat in Korea. We received many such requests, but this was very short notice. However, I told the party on the line that I would do the best I could to find one and would get back to them with my results. I headed off toward the officer's ward, not to slight the wounded enlisted men, but because Army officers were more trained in public speaking, and this was a short order.

I entered the officer's ward, and near the door standing around a bed with an amputee patient in it were two officers. I could hear them talking war talk as I approached. I was expecting to hear them talking about their experiences in Korea, but this sounded more like World War II. I had heard a couple of towns spoken of that were in France. I stepped forward and introduced myself. I said, "That sounds more like WWII than Korea." They all answered at the same time that it was WWII. I joined in then, and it turned out that the amputee officer in the bed was a tank commander and had been in my division, The 10th Armored and had been at Bastogne. The officer standing next to me introduced himself as Captain William Southwick of the 101st Paratroopers adding that he too had been at Bastogne.

As our conversation progressed it turned out that Capt. Southwick was the same officer who had come up to me as I lay on the stretcher on the doc's Jeep just outside of Bastogne. He was the one that had asked me if any of his men were still out there. The incident came back to both of us vividly. Capt. Southwick volunteered to be the speaker I needed that night. He was real fine, a spit and polish soldier with a chest full of ribbons from two wars and he was a great speaker. He and I became good friends, "Ole Bastogne Buddies," for many years.

THE ANGEL OF BASTOGNE

"The Angel of Bastogne," I had thought the vision I had of a pretty, young nurse back in the Battalion Aid Station in Bastogne, was only a figment of my delirium. However, it turns out that she was for real. She was Renee Lemaire, a young Belgium civilian nurse who had volunteered her services to help the wounded of the 20th Armored Infantry Battalion. To me she was like a faint but pleasant dream, and I can't tell you much about this brave and wonderful lady. Here is what two other members of the 20th AIB said about her.

Dr. Jack T. Prior, our Battalion Surgeon was the first to meet her. The following comments by Dr. Prior are taken from an article he wrote, "The Night Before Christmas – Bastogne, 1944," as it appeared in the Spring 2002 "Tiger Tales," the newsletter of the 10th Armored Division Veterans' Association.

"...I attempted to turn my litter bearers into bedside nursing personnel – they were assisted by the arrival at our station December 21st of two registered female civilian nurses. One of the nurses, Renee Lemaire, volunteered her services and the other girl was black, a native of the Belgium Congo. She was "willed" to me by her father and when we eventually left Bastogne he was most distraught with me for refusing to take her along. They played different roles among they dying. Renee shrank away from the fresh, gory trauma, while the Congo girl was always in the thick of the splinting, dressing and hemorrhage control. Renee preferred to circulate among the litter patients, sponging, feeding them and distributing the few medications we had (sulfa pills and plasma). The presence of these two girls was a morale factor of the highest order."

Dr. Prior goes on to describe his difficulties in providing medical care to so many wounded with so little to work with. He also tells of his visit to the 101st aid station in a riding hall. The next time he mentions Renee Lemaire was to tell of her efforts to try to get the parachutes after supply drops because she wanted the silk to make a wedding dress. He also states that, "She was invariably beaten out by a soldier and always returned empty handed."

On the evening of December 24th, Christmas Eve, Bastogne was bombed by German airplanes. Dr. Prior describes this experience with these words: "At 8:30 p.m. Christmas Eve, I was in a building next to my hospital preparing to go next door and write a letter for a young lieutenant to his wife. The lieutenant was dying of a chest wound. As I was about to step out of the door for the hospital one of my men asked me if I knew what day it was, pointing out that on Christmas Eve we should open a Champagne bottle. As the two of us filled our cups, the room, which was blackened out, became as bright as an arc welder's torch. Within a second or two we heard the screeching sound of the first bomb we had ever heard. Every bomb as it descends seems to be pointed right at you. We hit the floor as a terrible explosion next door rocked our building.

"I ran outside to discover that the three-story apartment serving as my hospital was a flaming pile of debris about six feet high. My men and I raced to the top of the debris and began flinging burning timbers aside looking for the wounded, some of which were shrieking for help. At this juncture the German Bomber, seeing the action, dropped down to strafe us with his machine guns. We slide under some vehicles, and he repeated this maneuver several times before leaving the area. A large number of men joined us, and we located a cellar window. Some men volunteered to be lowered into the smoking cellar on a rope and two or three injured were pulled out before the entire building fell into the cellar."

The doctor estimated that about twenty injured were killed in the bombing along with the nurse Renee Lemaire. He added that before his unit left Bastogne, most of the bodies had been recovered and identified including Renee Lemaire. Dr. Prior wrote, "I brought her remains to her parents encased in the white parachute she so dearly wanted." He also wrote the following commendation for her and forwarded it to the 10th Armored's commanding general but never heard if any action was taken.

Medical Detachment
205h Armored Infantry Battalion
APO 260, U.S. Army
1 January 1945

SUBJECT: Commendation for Renee Bernadette Emilie
Lemaire (Deceased)
TO: Commanding General,
10th Armored Division
APO 260, U.S. Army
(Attn: Division Surgeon)
Thru Channels.

As Battalion Surgeon, 20th Armored Infantry Battalion,
I am recommending a commendation for Renee Lemaire on the following evidence: This girl, a registered
nurse in the country of Belgium, volunteered her services at the aid station, 20th Armored Infantry Battalion
in Bastogne, Belgium, 21 December, 1944. At this time
the station was holding about 150 patients since the
city was encircled by enemy forces and evacuation
was impossible. Many of these patients were seriously
injured and in great need of immediate nursing attention. This girl cheerfully accepted the Herculean task
and worked without adequate rest or food until the
night of her untimely death on 24 December 1944.
She changed dressings, fed patients unable to feed
themselves, gave out medications, bathed and made
the patients more comfortable, and was of great assistance in the administration of plasma and other
professional duties. Her very presence among those
wounded men seemed to be an inspiration to those
whose morale had declined from prolonged suffering.
On the night of December 24 the building in which Renee Lemaire was working was scored with a direct hit
by an enemy bomber. She, together with those whom
she was caring for so diligently, were instantly killed.
It is on these grounds that I recommend the highest
award possible to one, who though not a member of

the armed forces of the Unites States, was of invaluable assistance to us.

JACK T PRIOR

Captain, MC

Commanding
Renee Bernadette Emilie Lemaire
Place du Carre 30
Bastogne, Belgium

The following is an article written by a sergeant who had met Nurse Renee Lemaire and witnessed the bombing of the aid station from his post across the street. It was written to "Tiger Tales" after he read the article by Dr. Prior.

More on Nurse Renee Lemaire
By William J. Kerby, 20th AI BN

When we pulled back from Noville to Bastogne, Captain Geiger informed me that we were now attached to the 101st Airborne Division. He stated that we were going into reserve and would be used when needed. He said to look for a billet for your men and to notify him of our whereabouts.

I found a nice three-story building with a big basement. The first floor was a 5 and 10 cent store with a large kitchen at the rear. The second and third floors were living quarters. While in the basement, we started a small fire with what we thought was play money that we found in the corner of the basement along with a broken chair. (About a month later, we found out that it was real money). Down the stairs came Dr. Naftulin and Nurse Renee Lemaire. He introduced her to me and said they were looking for a building that would serve as an aid station. They left for about fifteen minutes. When they returned, Dr. Naftulin said, "Sergeant, this basement would make an excellent aid station." I told him that was fine, and he could have it. I stated that I would take my men elsewhere to find another billet. We moved down and across the street about forty yards. The house was on the side of a hill. You could walk in the door from the roadside and go down a flight of stairs, walk in and out into the back-yard. There we dug foxholes and a latrine.

On Christmas Eve, we were told that the Germans had parachuted men in white uniforms around Bastogne. I posted guards at each corner of the building. My post was facing the aid station about thirty-five or forty yards away. All of a sudden the night sky was brighter than the Las Vegas strip from the magnesium flares that the German bomber pilots had dropped. A few seconds later, the first German bomber dropped his first bomb on the aid station, a direct hit. The second bomb landed in our backyard and wiped out all our empty foxholes, leaving only the latrine...Thanks God!!!! The second German bomber dropped down to strafe us with machine gun fire. All the GI's started to shoot at the plane with machine guns, rifles and car-bines. He dropped a bomb that was a direct hit on a building two doors from ours. That building just hap-pened to be a distillery. The bottles flew all over, and some were found two weeks later in the snow banks. I faced toward the aid station and Renee Lemaire was helping some wounded GI's out of the building. She went back in the building and came out helping more wounded yelling, "Help, help, water, water." The flames from the fire were intensifying. She was safe and sound out of the building but decide to go back in and help. Renee Lamaire never returned. The woman was a heroine and a saint. I am an eyewitness to these above facts.

In 1994, the 50th anniversary of Renee Lemaire's death a ceremony was held in Bastogne, Belgium, and a memorial plaque in her honor was placed on the building that now stands where the aid station had been. Dr. Prior was responsible for having this plaque placed in her honor where his hospital once stood. He and many other members of the 20th Armored Infantry Battalion will never forget this fine young lady.

Note: Renee Lemaire and the nurse from the Congo only served at the aid station of the 20th Infantry Battalion and not at the aid station of the 101st Airborne as shown on television.

Belgique News Release Regarding 1994 "Tiger" Tour

This column was printed in a Belgian newspaper and translated by Anne and Ned Norris, CCA, CCB.

The 10th U.S. Armored Division returns to Bastogne the 15th of this August.

The 10th American Armored Division was the first unit to experience the shock of the German attack at the beginning of the Battle of Bastogne. Its veterans will be honored the 15th of this August. The town of Bastogne will also pay tribute to the victims of the massacre at Noville and to the nurse Renee Lemaire who died on duty on Christmas Eve 1944.

While the Americans strained to consolidate the defense of Bastogne at the outbreak of the battle of the Ardennes, it was the men of the 10th Armored who were sent on the double to the outskirts of the town to set up roadblocks. To do this the 10th Armored organized three combat teams. Teams O'Hara, Cherry and Desobry were moved to Wardin, Longvilly and Noville to try to stop the 2nd Panzer and the 26th Volksgrenadier Divisions. These engagements were extremely violent. The Americans were forced to retreat, but their actions at these decisive hours of the battle held off the German attack. Our late colleague Joss Heinz described in his writing on the battle that the 10th Armored under the circumstances had suffered dramatic losses: 73 dead, 279 wounded, 116 disappeared or prisoners. Among the civilian victims it included 26 dead at Longvilly, 30 at Noville and 69 at Wardin. Besides there were 67 houses destroyed at Longvilly, 129 at Wardin and 39 at Noville.

To commemorate these battles at the outbreak of the war, the town of Bastogne has set up turrets of tanks of the 10th on the outskirts of town.

On this Monday the 15th of August the town will pay its respects to the veterans of this American unit who are returning to the Ardennes.

Also in this ceremony the authorities will recall the tragedy at Noville. After the departure of the 10th Armored it is known that a German suppression unit was brought into Noville. These Nazi killers in the pay of the Gestapo took some 20 hostages. At random they selected 20 victims who were shot behind the church. These included the priest Louis Delvaux (45), the teacher Auguste Lutgen (45), brothers François and Felix Deprez (30 and 35), Joseph Rosier (35), Romain Henquinet (42) and Roger Beaujean (21). Besides the village inhabitants a subject of the Grand Duchy Michel Stranen from Troine was also killed by these Gestapo men probably the same ones who murdered some 30 hostages in this same period. On the 15th of August Bastogne will also highlight the heroic figure of Renee Lemaire, a young nurse killed by German bombs on Christmas Eve. The 24th of December, enemy aviation heavily bombed the center of Bastogne itself. One projectile completely demolished the military aid station that the Americans had set up in the basement of the Sarma Store on the rue de Neufchate. The volunteer nurse, Renee Lemaire from Bastogne managed to evacuate six soldiers from the burning building. She died while she tried to save a seventh wounded.

Printed in the United States
By Bookmasters